THE PLAINS OF

NORWICH

Richard Lane

The Larks Press

Published by the Larks Press,
Ordnance Farmhouse, Guist Bottom,
Dereham, Norfolk NR20 5PF

Printed at the Lanceni Press, Garrood Drive, Fakenham

March 1999

British Library Cataloguing-in-Publication Data
A catalogue record for this book is available at the British
Library

ACKNOWLEDGEMENTS

Photographs of Agricultural Hall Plain c. 1890s; St Andrew's Hall
Plain 1896; St Benedict's Plain; St Paul's Church; Theatre Royal
c. 1920s; Edward Boardman; Cotman's drawing of Earlham Hall,
and the portrait of John Crome reproduced by courtesy of
Norfolk County Council Library and Information Service.
Photographs of the South African War Memorial c.1910 and St
Stephen's Plain c.1890, reproduced by kind permission of author
and historian, Neil Storey.
Thanks also to Terence J. Burchell for copying all the historical
photographs and to David Shiret for permission to use his
drawing of St George's Colegate.

Maps at the beginning of each chapter have been reproduced
from the 1883 Ordnance Survey Map.

ISBN 0 948400 77 3

WHAT ARE THE PLAINS?

During my childhood in the early 1950s, the wide concrete pavement fronting the row where my parents had their shop, was referred to by young and old alike as the plain. It was quite natural, a part of everyday speech, an expression for an open space no matter how large or small.

For centuries plain has been the word used by the inhabitants of Norwich to define the squares and open spaces amidst the narrow maze of streets. Nicholas Sotherton, in his account of Kett's Rebellion written during the 1550s, described fighting between the rebels and Lord Northampton's forces 'in the playne before the Pallace gate of the Bishop', a reference to St Martin at Palace Plain from over 400 years ago.

Some writers have suggested that it is a term peculiar to Norwich, but it does appear to have a wider use in both Norfolk and Suffolk. Great Yarmouth has several plains: Church, Brewery and Priory to name but three. William White's *Directory of Norfolk* published in 1845 mentions the first and also Theatre Plain. The market town of Holt has a Shirehall Plain still shown on a street sign and listed in *White's Directory* published over a century and a half ago. Loddon has a Church Plain while over the border in Suffolk there is a Royal Plain in Lowestoft and a St Margaret's Plain in Ipswich.

The plains were (and the surviving ones still are) distinctive areas, part of the overall street plan, enabling the inhabitants to identify where they lived or worked. Just as other towns and cities have named squares, so Norwich has its plains.

Maps, directories, books and personal reminiscences from the older generation have enabled me to locate a total of fifteen named plains in the city. Only five are officially marked by street signs: Agricultural Hall, Bank, St Catherine's, St Martin at Palace and St Mary's.

1

Maddermarket, Redwell, St Andrew's Hall, St Benedict's, St Giles, St George's, St Margaret's, St Paul's, St Stephen's and Theatre are not marked. St Andrew's, however, still appears on maps and is used in the address of both Garsett House and St Andrew's Hall. St George's Plain remains in current use as the address of Radio Broadland and in the recent development of the old Norvic shoe factory. St Paul's, often referred to as a square, has disappeared; so, too, has Theatre Plain owing to the demolition of surrounding buildings and street widening. Redwell has lost its identity to Bank Plain.

A. W. Morant's map of the city published in 1873 shows All Saints' Plain instead of Green. I have found no other evidence to support this, but in his defence, and using the word in its local descriptive sense, the area is certainly a plain. It is a matter of name but most sources going back to the early years of the nineteenth century call it All Saint's Green.

All the plains so far mentioned lie within the historic core of the city as defined by the circuit of its walls. Norwich has, however, grown, spreading beyond its medieval flint boundaries, absorbing neighbouring hamlets and villages. One such hamlet is Earlham, where, in a country setting, overlooking the river Yare, lies University Plain, Norwich's newest, a twentieth century creation.

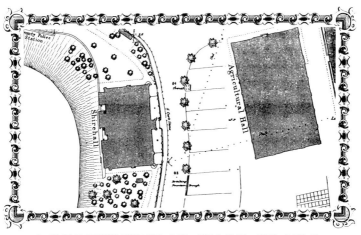

AGRICULTURAL HALL PLAIN

Prince of Wales Road was opened for public traffic on 9th November 1862 to create a direct and somewhat grandiose link between the city centre and Thorpe Station. It was to be an impressive introduction to Norwich for rail travellers; a wide, sweeping curve flanked by fine buildings. Unfortunately, the scheme ran out of money, the work was curtailed and only the city end was really developed as originally envisaged. Prince of Wales Terrace (1865) curving along the northern side of the bend gives some idea of the planner's ambitions. Occupied today by solicitors and estate agents, this fine terrace has retained some of the ironwork on the balconies. Steps, enclosed by iron railings, lead down to basement entrances, once the below-stairs world of maids, cooks and butlers.

Agricultural Hall Plain, although given its own separate identity on a street sign, is regarded as being part of Prince of Wales Road. (Anglia Television gives its address as Prince of Wales Road). It stands on quite a steep incline; a natural rise in the ground has been exaggerated by the remains of one of the earth embankments which formed the outer defences of Norwich Castle. Attempts have been made in the past to reduce the gradient with only moderate success.

The Agricultural Hall recalls the days when the city was an important centre for the region's farmers. Until 1960, when it was removed to Hall Road on the outskirts, the Cattle Market created a great semicircle of livestock every Saturday around the foot of the

3

Castle Mound from the Agricultural Hall to Farmer's Avenue. Only in recent years with the development of Castle Mall and a general refurbishment of the entire area has visible evidence of the old Cattle Market been swept away. Now only Farmer's Avenue, Cattle Market Street and Market Avenue recall the days when livestock was brought to the very heart of a busy city.

Agricultural Hall not far from the site of the old Cattle Market

Designed by Norwich architect J. B. Pearce, the red brick Agricultural Hall was opened in 1882 by the Prince of Wales (later King Edward VII). The main hall was 147 feet in length and 98 feet wide, equipped with removable wrought-iron pens to contain the livestock. On three sides of the hall were galleries and at the east and west ends cranes were situated to raise and lower large exhibits. In the basement was a kitchen and a dining room; on the ground floor a buffet, ladies' room and a boardroom together with the secretary's and other administrative offices. Over the main entrance was a room 97 feet by 48 feet containing a stage which could be used for public assemblies such as lectures or political meetings.

Licensed for theatrical and other forms of entertainment, the building was put to a wide range of uses. Military tattoos were staged in the main hall. Charles Blondin, the great French acrobat, guided a man across the hall on a tightrope suspended above the heads of the audience. One of the giant figures of Victorian politics, William Gladstone, made a speech there.

My father can recall the main hall being used for general trade shows in the 1920s and 1930s. He also told me that the fun-fairs which covered the old Cattle Market at Christmas and Easter actually overlapped into the hall; roundabouts and dodgem car rides were set up under its roof. It was also used as a skating-rink where roller-skates with rubber wheels could be hired. Today it remains very much a place of entertainment being the home of Anglia Television.

A hundred years after the hall was opened, Anglia completed an office extension at the back. Before building work actually began, the site was excavated in 1979 and the remains of an Anglo-Saxon timber church and graveyard, hitherto unknown, were uncovered. Archaeologists believe that this little church existed for around seventy-five years, only to be destroyed by the Normans to make way for the north-eastern bailey of Norwich Castle.

The Agricultural Hall does seem a trifle drab in comparison to its much grander, neo-classical neighbour. Faced in limestone, it has a projecting balcony and a splendid portico with eight coupled columns of the Ionic order. Like some Greek or Roman temple that has somehow come unscathed through the ravages of the centuries, it faces the busy flow of present-day traffic. It is not hard to imagine figures in flowing togas climbing the steps on their way to devotions, until, that is, the eye catches the words POST OFFICE in bold relief beneath the sculptured crown on the pediment. The illusion is broken, no classical gods have ever been worshipped there.

Hardwick House, once Harvey & Hudson's Crown Bank

Now also a part of Anglia Television, Hardwick House began life as a bank. The sculptured crown signified Harvey and Hudson's Crown Bank which moved from more modest premises at 19 King Street, into this splendid, purpose-built temple of banking costing £13,000. It is one of the few surviving buildings designed by Philip Hardwick (1792-1870) and opened its doors to customers on 1st January 1866. Four years later the bank collapsed into bankruptcy; Sir Robert Harvey had, as R. H. Mottram put it, backed France in the Franco-Prussian War. But there was more to it than that. Sir Robert had been free in his use of the bank's deposits by gambling on the Stock Exchange. Sums such as £5,000 of the City Council's money; £6,000 held for the Norwich Board of Guardians; £2,000 of county money, and £70,000 belonging to one of his sleeping partners, were all lost. When the facts emerged in

**Agricultural Hall Plain in the 1890s
before the Royal Hotel was built**

1870, Sir Robert committed suicide in the garden of his home, Crown Point, on the Trowse Hall estate. The bank's total deficit amounted to £400,000. It then merged with Gurney's Bank on Bank Plain.

In 1875, the Norwich Post Master, Benjamin Viny Winch, persuaded the Government to move the Post Office from its site at the bottom of Exchange Street into the former bank. He was to manage the new office for sixteen years until his death in 1891 at the age of 60.

Additions and improvements were subsequently made extending the building along King Street. By the 1930s, however, it was becoming clear that a new sorting office would have to be specially built to cope with the increasing quantity of mail. In 1937, a site was acquired on Thorpe Road, but the outbreak of war two years later curtailed all work on the scheme.

In 1943, part of the sorting operation (parcels and inland letters) was moved into the Agricultural Hall which was leased from Norwich Corporation on a temporary basis. Work did not begin on the Thorpe Road sorting office until early in 1955 and it was only ready for use in October 1957, twenty years after the site had been acquired.

The Head Post Office finally moved out of Hardwick House in 1969 and for a few years the building stood empty. Plans were made to convert it into flats and offices but it was then taken over by Anglia Television who needed to expand their operation. In the early 1980s a glazed link was built across the intervening Crown Road, blocking the thoroughfare and uniting two very diverse nineteenth century buildings.

At the top of the plain, splitting the junction with Market Avenue, rises the symbolic figure of peace represented by a bronze angel with outstretched wings placing the sword of conflict into her sheath. Designed by Messrs G. and F. Wade, this memorial of Aberdeen granite, Portland stone and bronze cost around £1,600 and was unveiled in 1904. On it are recorded the names of 300 officers and men of the city and county who lost their lives in the South African Wars.

The South African War Memorial c. 1910

7

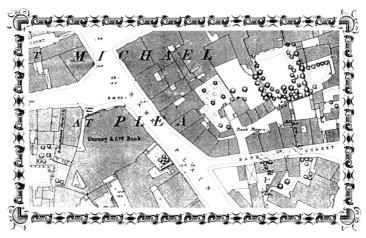

BANK PLAIN (AND REDWELL PLAIN)

The derivation of the name is quite obvious. The entire western side of the plain is taken up by Barclay's Bank, a substantial, neo-Georgian building dating from 1929, designed by the firm of Norwich architects, E. Boardman and Son, whose offices were in Old Bank of England Court, Queen Street. The interior is spectacular, consisting of a large apsed hall, almost cathedral-like in its proportions. It would certainly have won the approval of E. T. Boardman's late father and founder of the firm, whose designs greatly influenced the architectural appearance of Norwich during the nineteenth and early twentieth centuries.

Bank Plain has its origins in the eighteenth century, when Gurney's Bank, to which Barclay's can trace at least one of its roots, stood on this site. John and Henry Gurney founded the bank in 1775. Henry's son Bartlett moved the banking house from Pitt Street to Number 3 Redwell Plain in 1777, taking over larger premises which had once belonged to a wine merchant. The building occupied a part of the site on which Barclay's now stands. R. H. Mottram gives an accurate and affectionate portrait of the early days of the bank in his novel *Our Mr Dormer* published in 1927. The city may be called Easthampton, the bank's owners, John and Joseph Doughty, but it was Norwich and Gurney's Bank which formed the basis of his story.

The Gurney family had amassed a considerable fortune in the

8

The original Gurney's Bank from which Bank Plain took its name

worsted weaving industry, and as Quakers were renowned for integrity in all their business and personal dealings. Expansion followed, and within seven years of its foundation branches had been established in Yarmouth, King's Lynn, Wisbech and Halesworth in a move unusual for a county bank at that time. Links with Barclay's were forged when Richard Gurney, who joined in 1779, married the only daughter of London banker, David Barclay.

In those days, London Street, Redwell Street, Queen Street and Blue Boar Lane merged into a square called Redwell Plain. Part of the plain can still be made out where London Street widens at its junction with Bank Plain. The extension to St Andrew's Street to create a direct route for trams at the turn of the century, altered the configuration and Blue Boar Lane seems to have disappeared into the wide thoroughfare that now forms Bank Plain.

White's *Directory of Norfolk* published in 1845 mentions both Redwell Plain and Bank Plain. The former has fallen out of use while the latter is marked on a street sign and is the official address of all the businesses situated there.

Like Anglia Television, the former Royal Hotel used to give its address as Prince of Wales Road rather than Agricultural Hall Plain. Yet when it was built towards the end of the last century, it seems to have been deemed a part of Bank Plain which is why I have included it in this section of the book.

Royal Hotel

It took over both the name and the licence of the Royal Hotel in Gentleman's Walk, one of a number of long, narrow coaching inns which looked out on to the Market Place. In 1899, the inn was transformed by architect George Skipper (1856-1948) into the Royal Arcade, leaving only the original hotel façade above the entrance of this art nouveau gem of a late Victorian shopping mall.

Edward Boardman (1833-1910) was the architect of the present Royal Hotel building. This influential and highly creative man designed a delightfully eccentric hotel, reminiscent in many ways of a scaled-down château which has been lifted from the French countryside and set down in the centre of Norwich. Yet for all its continental feel, with ornate turrets and battlements, the deep red and highly decorative brickwork is local, known as Costesseyware, made by Guntons of Costessey. It was popular among local architects of the time because the bricks could be rubbed and shaped into patterns, some of most delicate intricacy, and were used on a number of public buildings including the Norfolk and Norwich Hospital.

Edward Boardman

The Royal Hotel opened in 1897. Modern, spacious, luxurious, it became the premier hotel of Norwich, completely the opposite of its cramped, rambling eighteenth century forbear on Gentleman's Walk. In some ways, however, both hotels have ultimately shared a similar fate. Whereas one became a shopping arcade, the other has become an office block but not without a threat to its very existence. During the 1970s, the owners of the Royal Hotel sought permission to demolish and rebuild, but fortunately Boardman's gothic extravaganza was saved by the City Planning Department.

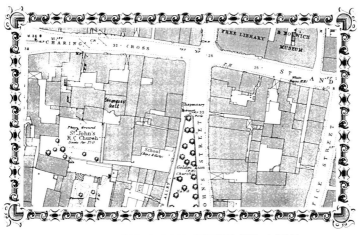

MADDERMARKET PLAIN

In 1845, a toy dealer by the name of Thomas Boswell, and a chemist and druggist called James Spatchett were listed as having their premises on Maddermarket Plain. Amongst all the various sources consulted, these two references are the only ones that name it as a plain in print. The compilers of *White's Directory* were probably following what both Boswell and Spatchett had told them.

Nestling in the shadow of St John Maddermarket Church, this little square with its narrow ways retains some of the atmosphere of the old plains. Only the northern side, opening on to Charing Cross and St Andrew's Street with the wide vista of Duke Street opposite, allows the light into this shady quarter.

Maddermarket...Charing Cross...these names bear witness to the textile trade which for centuries was the dominant industry of Norwich. Throughout the central part of the city, beside the river Wensum, the cloth dyers lived and worked. Enrolled Deeds for 1285 and 1311 show evidence of a distinct grouping of these workers in the Westwick Street area. The eastern part of this street was once known as Letestere Row which means Lister's or Dyer's Row. In 1681, for example, the quarter around what is now Duke Street was a clutter of 'tradesmen's and dyers' houses who foul the river water by their constant washing and cleaning of their cloth.' (Baskerville)

The Maddermarket was the place where those dyers

purchased the Turkey-red dye, made from the roots of the plant *rubia tinctorum*, known as the madder root. Charing Cross is a corruption of Shereshill, Shergate or Shereman, after the shearers who trimmed the nap of the cloth.

'St John's, Maddermarket,' wrote William White, 'is an ancient, but handsome church founded before the survey made in Edward the Confessor's reign and dedicated to the Holy Trinity and St John the Baptist.' This is slightly misleading, suggesting that the present church dates from that period. As with nearly all of the city's surviving churches, rebuilding and restoration took place over the centuries. St John's is in the Perpendicular style dating from the fifteenth century though there is some evidence of fourteenth century work. W. H. Claxton in his *Record of Local Events in Norwich, From 575 to 1904* stated: '1310. Church of St John Maddermarket built.' The north aisle, according to Arthur Mee in the Norfolk volume of *The King's England* (1951), stands 'on the site of a church built perhaps in Saxon days.'

The rebuilding of the church on a grander scale appears to have blocked the lane (St John's Alley) necessitating the creation of an arched passage through the base of the tower.

Passage through St John's tower

Inside is a fine array of brasses, the earliest dating from 1412 commemorating Walter Noneslee and his wife. There are also memorials to the wealthy and influential Sotherton family. Leonard, whose substantial home is the Strangers' Hall Museum (closed at the time of writing), was Mayor of Norwich in 1539. His brother Nicholas wrote an eyewitness account of Kett's Rebellion of 1549.

The church is now maintained by the Redundant Churches Fund with money provided by Parliament, the Church of England and by gifts from the public. Although no longer used for worship it remains consecrated and is open three days a week.

High on the wall between the north aisle arches is a memorial to Lady Margaret, Duchess of Norfolk. Lord John Howard of Walden erected it in 1791 to the memory of his ancestor, who had died in 1563 while staying in the Duke of Norfolk's Palace which stood almost opposite Maddermarket Plain. A green plaque affixed to the wall of St Andrew's multi-storey car park says: 'One of the largest town houses in England stood near this site 1561-1711.'

Built between 1561 and 1563, it stood in an area which any present-day estate agent would hardly describe as desirable, surrounded as it was by the cloth workers. But the Duke of Norfolk wanted to build his palace close to the city centre on what appears to have been the only available site.

'It was rebuilt on a larger and more splendid plan in 1672 by Henry, Duke of Norfolk,' wrote William White. Apparently some of the building material was taken from St Benet's Abbey, the remains of which stand in an isolated marshland spot beside the river Bure near Ludham.

Further rebuilding took place during the 1670s and 1680s. William White described it as 'a large quadrangular mansion... Among its accommodation for amusement, were a theatre, tennis court, and covered bowling alley; the latter said to have been the largest in England.'

As has already been noted, it hardly stood in the most desirable of locations. The river was fouled by residue from the dyers and fullers whose houses hemmed the palace in. Thomas Baskerville, writing in 1681, described his visit there: 'We rowed under 5 or 6 bridges, and then landed at the Duke of Norfolk's Palace, a sumptuous new-built house not yet finished within, but seated in a dung-hole place, though it had cost the Duke already 30

The Duke's Palace in Cleere's map of 1696

thousand pounds on building...for it hath but little room for gardens and is pent upon all sides both on this and the other side of the river, with tradesmen's and dyers houses .'

Thirty years later, in 1711, demolition of this great town house began at the hands of the Duke himself. Three years previously he had quarrelled with the Mayor, Thomas Havers, who, on behalf of the city, had objected to the form of a pageant proposed by the Duke. The Mayor 'refused his company of comedians to enter the city with trumpets &c.' In his anger, the Duke of Norfolk 'defaced' his palace and abandoned it.

One wing remained after its demolition, later leased to the Court of Guardians as a workhouse; other parts of the site were used as a common staithe. A fragment survived into the present century forming part of the Duke's Palace Inn until its demolition in 1968. Fortunately for posterity, the historian Kirkpatrick made a drawing of the palace in 1710, and in 1974 part of the foundations were excavated and mapped. All trace has now gone; the multi-storey car park and telephone exchange cover the site and only the name Duke Street and the official green plaque give any clues as to the past splendours of this site.

When, in 1563, Lady Margaret's body was carried the short distance from the palace to the church for burial in the north aisle, a great procession of civic and church dignitaries, lords and ladies, filed solemnly across the plain. No doubt the cortège was watched by a large crowd, too. She was, after all, the second wife of one of the foremost noblemen in England.

Fifteen years later, the Maddermarket was the scene of another and even grander procession. In 1578, the Mayor and Corporation were informed that 'her Majesty designed a progress through Norfolk and Suffolk, and to visit this city.'

Preparations for Queen Elizabeth I's visit started in June, two months before she was due to arrive. St Stephen's Gate was refurbished, streets repaired and tidied. The wall of St John's Maddermarket churchyard was taken down and rebuilt in order to widen the narrow street down which she was due to pass on her way from the Market Place to the Cathedral. The Queen was in Norwich from 16th until 22nd August and lodged at the Bishop's Palace. During her stay she was 'entertained with splendid *pageantries,* principally allied to the trade and manufactures of the city.'

14

By the eighteenth century, the Maddermarket had become the scene of a market in human labour - the hirings. Young people waited on the plain hoping to hire themselves out as unskilled assistants to tradesmen or as domestic servants to families. In 1781, 13 year old John Crome, later to become one of the city's most famous artists, stood in the shadow of St John's Church awaiting the chance of employment.

At the foot of the churchyard the parish pump still stands though bereft of its handle. It was probably the work of William Shalders whose premises in 1845 were on Bank Plain. He was described in *White's Directory* as a leather merchant and patent fountain pump manufacturer. His son, William Shalders junior, was listed as a hydraulics engineer and leather worker.

The pump was used to fill the spraying carts and as a source of drinking water. What effect it had on the stomachs of the local population hardly bears thinking about when you consider that the pump stands on sloping ground just below the churchyard. No wonder the first public analyst of Norwich was moved to declare that the water was 'pure essence of churchyard.'

Maddermarket Plain from Charing Cross

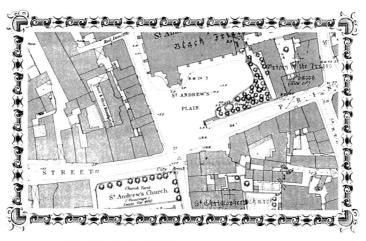

ST ANDREW'S HALL PLAIN

Before St Andrew's Street was extended to create a direct link with Bank Plain, it ended in the large square outside St Andrew's and Blackfriars' Hall. The main thoroughfare continued along Princes Street to Tombland. In order to reach Bank Plain, a sharp right turn was involved from Prince's Street into Redwell Street. Public transport in the form of the city's tram system took priority and in 1899 St Andrew's Street was extended, at the expense of several properties, to Bank Plain with the sweeping incline we have today.

Like many of the plains, it was a meeting of the ways: St George's Street crossing the river to the old ward Over-the-Water; St Andrew's Hill leading up to London Street; Prince's Street, formerly Hungate, a name which lives on in the small church (now a museum) of St Peter Hungate at the top of Elm Hill. And St Andrew's Street, once called Wymer, then St Andrew's Broad Street while it was still narrow. The word 'Broad' has ironically disappeared from what is now quite a wide street.

William White in 1845 listed the square simply as St Andrew's Plain; a difference which remains to this day. The official address of Garsett House is St Andrew's Hall Plain, but the Hall itself, according to address details given in the current telephone directory, is on St Andrew's Plain. There are no street signs to solve this minor anomaly.

The church of St Andrew at the south west corner of the plain (although officially on St Andrew's Street) is the second largest in the city after St Peter Mancroft. It is widely regarded as being one of the best examples of East Anglian medieval architecture. Of pre-Conquest foundation, St Andrew's was rebuilt on a larger scale during the later years of the fifteenth century. The tower, 96 feet high, was completed in 1477 and the remainder of the church in 1506.

Inside is an inscription which, according to Arthur Mee in *The King's England*, bears 'the thrilling name of Abraham Lincolne of 1758, perhaps an uncle of the American President.' Lincoln could certainly trace his ancestry back to Norfolk but the most tangible of his roots actually lie in Hingham and Swanton Morley.

Some of the finest memorials in the city are to be found in St Andrew's, notably those commemorating the Suckling family. Robert Suckling is depicted on a wall monument kneeling in prayer facing his wife, their children behind them. The largest is a canopied tomb to his son, Sir John Suckling, who died in 1613. He is depicted as an armoured figure reclining, with his head supported by his right arm, and looking down at his wife lying beside him. One son kneels at the head, another at the foot, while on the front four figures representing his daughters kneel in prayer.

Robert's name lives on in the house which bears his name to the east of the church. Suckling House is now Cinema City and is a blend of medieval, Tudor and Georgian. The earliest part, the banqueting hall, dates from the fourteenth century. Although the house is named after Robert Suckling, a circular plaque high on the wall lists previous occupants and shows that a dwelling has stood on this spot since at least the late thirteenth century.

'Wm de Rollesby 1285; John Fairchild bailiff 1331; John Parlet MP bailiff 1380; John Cambridge Mayor 1494; John Clerk MP Mayor 1507; Robert Suckling MP Mayor 1564; Lived here.'

Suckling House was restored and given to the city in 1924 by Ethel and Helen Colman, members of the Norfolk family whose fame and fortune was founded on the manufacture of mustard. It was subsequently used as a lecture hall, as a venue for school prize-givings and as a meeting-place. In 1927 it was the scene of the inaugural meeting of the Round Table founded in Norwich by Louis Marchesi.

Opposite Suckling House and occupying a prominent corner

position between Prince's Street and St Andrew's Street, is Garsett House, a timber-framed building dating from 1589. Also known as Armada House, a local tradition says that timbers used in its construction were salvaged from ships of the Spanish Armada which were wrecked off the East Anglian coast. High on the south wall, facing Suckling House, the plaster relief of a galleon commemorates the event.

Garsett House

A dwelling has stood on this site since the fourteenth century. John de Norweigh, John Pirremund, Adam Baas (1373), Robert Dilham (1495), William Crane (1505) are some of its recorded occupants. By 1570, Robert Garsett was in residence. He rebuilt it and his name has been linked to the house ever since. Sheriff of Norwich in 1599, he died in March 1611; a marble monument consisting of his bust and effigies of his son Robert and daughter Elizabeth is in St Andrew's Church.

In the 1860s a school, Sunderland House, occupied the premises. Later in the century, solicitor Alfred Kent set up his practice in Garsett House which was eventually taken over by his son. Ernest Kent was a noted antiquarian and on his death bequeathed the old house to the Norfolk and Norwich Archaeological Society who set up their library and headquarters on the first floor. Today it also houses the Norfolk Archaeological Unit which is part of the Norfolk Museums Service.

Unfortunately, Victorian town planners took their toll of

Garsett House towards the end of the last century. Part of the southern wing was demolished in 1898 when St Andrew's Street was extended to make way for the trams; which gives this splendid old building an oddly truncated look.

St Andrew's and Blackfriars' Hall once formed the nave and chancel respectively of the great conventual church of St John the Baptist. Built by the Dominican or Black Friars, work was finally completed in 1471 after fire had partly destroyed their building in 1413. A green plaque on the wall states that the nave was built at the expense of Sir Thomas Erpingham (1357-1428) `Warrior of Agincourt'.

Only sixty-eight years after its completion, this fine church was in danger of going the way of many other such religious houses when Henry VIII set about dissolving the monasteries. Augustine Steward, three times Mayor of Norwich, whose lopsided house still

St Andrew's Hall today.
A surviving 17th century print shows a tall priest's house built in front of the first window on the left and the barrel, on which the friars stood to preach, in front of the furthest window on the right. The preaching-yard was a popular gathering-place in the early evening in late medieval times.

19

stands on Tombland, was instrumental in saving the Blackfriars' Convent from destruction. Through his efforts, the City Corporation bought the building in 1539 for £80 from Henry's commissioners. The nave (St Andrew's Hall) was to be, in the words of the petition to the King, 'a fayer and large hall, well pathed, for the Mayor and his brethrene, with all the citizens of the same to repair thereunto for their common assemblages as often as shall be expedient.'

It was money well spent for St Andrew's and Blackfriars' Hall, despite some heavy restoration work by T. Barry the City Surveyor in 1863, stands as one of the finest examples of friary architecture in the country. The one part missing is a handsome octagonal tower which fell down in 1712.

The chancel (Blackfriars' Hall) was for many years known as the 'Dutch Church', a place of worship for the Dutch community in Norwich. During Elizabeth I's reign some 5,000 Flemish Protestants took refuge in Norwich to escape the vicious régime imposed on the Netherlands by Spain's barbaric general, the Duke of Alva. These 'Strangers', as the refugees were called, proved of great benefit to the city because of the new weaving skills they brought with them. One of their number, Anthony de Solempne set up the city's first printing press in 1567.

Both Halls are still widely used for trade shows, exhibitions, political rallies, concerts, civic banquets, masonic meetings, balls and the eagerly awaited Norfolk and Norwich Beer Festival. Royalty has also been lavishly entertained in St Andrw's Hall: Edward VII, George V and George VI. It was there, too, that Charles II knighted Sir Thomas Browne.

The restored crypt is a coffee bar and the remains of the old cloisters can still be viewed. Blackfriars' Hall has a splendid collection of portraits of former civic dignitaries stretching back over the centuries.

St Andrew's Hall Plain, described by eyewitness Nicholas Sotherton as 'the Hyll next the corner late the Black Fryers', was the scene of fighting during Kett's Rebellion. On the afternoon of Saturday 24th August 1549, as the Earl of Warwick's forces gained entry into the city, the rebels re-grouped ready to mount counter-attacks. Warwick's soldiers did not know Norwich and easily became lost in the network of narrow streets. Already some of his baggage wagons carrying guns and ammunition, had missed the turning at Charing Cross to the Market Place and had ended up in Bishopgate where they fell into rebel hands.

Those rebels still inside the city split into three groups, using as their assembly points St Michael at Plea Church, St Simon and St Jude Church at the bottom of Elm Hill, and St Andrew's Hall. From these places they harassed the Royal troops.

In an attempt to disperse them, Warwick himself took charge of a force, moving from their temporary headquarters in the Market Place down through the Maddermarket and right into St Andrew's Street. There they were met by a hail of arrows fired by the rebels on St Andrew's Hall Plain. Fortunately for Warwick, Captain Drury, who had been in pursuit of the baggage wagons, returned along Princes Street with a company of harquebusiers (the harquebus was an early form of musket) and fired a volley into the rear of the rebel lines. The subsequent fighting was fierce and 300 were killed.

Once all the rebels had retreated to their camp on Mousehold, and the city was under Warwick's control, he set about billeting his troops. Many camped in the Market Place while his officers and other members of the gentry were found rooms in various houses. St Andrew's Hall became a stable for the army's horses and remained so until 7th September when the victorious Royal forces finally left the city.

St Andrew's Hall Plain in 1896

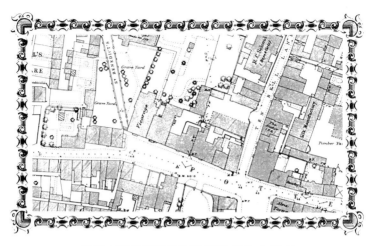

ST BENEDICT'S PLAIN

White's Directory makes no mention of St Benedict's Plain in 1845, but it is one that lives on in the memories of local authors who have written about the changing face of Norwich over the last century. One writer has confined it to the square at the junction of Pottergate (the street of the potters), Willow Lane, Cow Hill and Ten Bell Lane. Others have defined it as the widening of Pottergate from Ten Bell Lane westwards and the square created by the configuration of two groups of houses, several of which have gone.

Number 106 Pottergate stood on the southern side at right angles to the street, almost mirrored by 107 on the north side. Although they did not close the thoroughfare, they created a definite square, St Benedict's Plain. From old photographs and written descriptions, it seems that gabled houses faced the plain, making it a favourite spot among artists.

Progress in the destructive guise of road building and slum-clearance began to threaten this delightful but crowded area in the 1930s. A relief road for St Benedict's was planned in 1936 which would have cut across part of the plain. Number 107, said to be one of the oldest houses in Norwich, together with its immediate neighbours on the north side, was scheduled for demolition. Valiant efforts were made to save them, but the City Council won the day and part of the city's heritage was lost for a road which was never built. The war interrupted such schemes and, with the peace, plans changed.

Sadly, it does seem that 107 and its Tudor neighbours would have been lost anyway, because this densely-populated district was heavily bombed on 27th and 29th April 1942. Number 106, shaken to its foundation by the bombing, was declared unsafe and had to be demolished. Number 104, dating from 1687, survived and together with 102 and 100 (nineteenth century) make a pleasant grouping of houses, all that now remains of St Benedict's Plain.

Kinghorn House

A stone plaque on the wall of Number 104 records that Joseph Kinghorn, minister of St Mary's Baptist Church, lived there from 1789 until 1832. He was 24 when he arrived in Norwich which he described as 'an old comically built place.' A bachelor, scholar and painstaking student of the Bible, he was described as having a fine presence and great ministerial power. Later in his ministry, he established Sunday evening meetings which had never before been held in Norwich. He died in 1832 after forty-three years as pastor and is buried in the vaults of St Mary's Baptist Church on St Mary's Plain.

In 1822 the Eye Infirmary began its life in a building on St Benedict's Plain. Founded by 'three medical gentlemen', Lewis Evans, Robert Hull and Thomas Martineau, its charitable funds in 1845 only allowed 'accommodation for eight or nine in-patients, though it relieves annually about 300 out-patients, at the cost of about £200.' In 1854 it moved to other premises in Pottergate,

**The corner of St Benedict's Plain before the
demolition of the 1930s**

then, in 1913, to St Stephen's Road, opposite the Norfolk and
Norwich Hospital with which it was amalgamated in 1925.

Just to the north of the plain, between Pottergate and St
Benedict's Street, densely-packed courtyard and terrace houses once
crowded around the church from which the plain derived its name.
The air raids of April 1942 were some of the heaviest of the war,
reducing the area to rubble in a storm of fire and high explosives.
Life, however, soon returned. Prefabs were erected to provide
temporary houses which remained in place until 1970.

By 1974, a new development of flats and houses bordering the
plain had replaced the prefabs. Wellington Green and Ten Bell
Court were designed by Edward Skipper, son of George Skipper.
The central feature of this pleasant development is the tower of St
Benedict's. The rest of the church was destroyed during the air raids
but the round tower survived, scarred but intact, which says much
for the strength of Norman workmanship.

William White described the church as 'a small ancient edifice'. *Kelly's Directory* of 1937 said it was 'an ancient building of flint, in the Early English style, consisting of chancel, nave, north aisle, north and south porches and a round tower with octagonal belfry stage containing 3 bells.'

The church in its final form dated largely from the fifteenth century. According to Noel Spencer and Arnold Kent in *The Old Churches of Norwich*, the octagonal belfry stage may have been added at that time, although other sources suggest a century earlier. St Benedict's was, however, of much older foundation. Archaeological excavations during 1972 uncovered evidence of three more building stages in the church's history. The earliest dated from the late eleventh century, consisting of a small semicircular chancel and a nave. Around a century later, the chancel was enlarged, its end made square and the round tower added. Further rebuilding took place in the fourteenth century when all except the tower was demolished and replaced by a larger structure with nave and chancel of equal width. The fifteenth century saw the last complete rebuilding of St Benedict's. Modifications were subsequently made and in 1869 £180 was spent on repairs and a new roof. Twenty-seven years later, with an elderberry tree growing out of the tower, the church had become 'dilapidated and dangerous' and urgent repairs were carried out.

Arthur Mee, in 1940, described it as 'a neat little building of Norman and medieval days.' Within two years it had been destroyed.

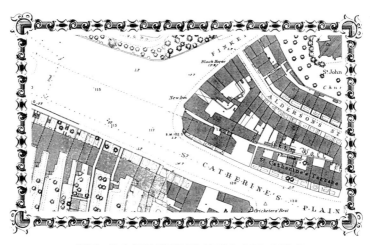

ST CATHERINE'S PLAIN

Names such as Alderson's Buildings, Gloucester Place, Kensington Place, Lakenham Hall Road, Oxford Street, Surrey Street, and Finket Street were all linked to St Catherine's Plain by William White in 1845. Today, Finklegate forms a junction with Queen's Road, while the southern end of Surrey Street has been realigned to form its own separate junction with Queen's Road. Between the two junctions a small garden has been created with grass and shrubs adding a pleasant touch to the area.

St Catherine's Plain is still preserved on a street sign and today is confined to the area between the junctions. In the nineteenth century, however, it appears to have been a street in its own right, continuing the thoroughfare from Queen's Road, which then ended at the Surrey Street/Finklegate junction, to Bracondale at the junction with City Road and Ber Street. Just as with some of the other plains, the changing face of Norwich has altered its identity completely, so that the original extent of St Catherine's Plain has been absorbed by Queen's Road, leaving only the name and a fragment.

In 1845, it was a separately defined part of the city, the address of a small academy run by Charlotte Hunt. There were two bakers and flour dealers, Francis Boulton and the appropriately named Jonathan Pye, and a horse dealer called Robert Ward. Eleanor Crowe was a milliner, William Wordingham a joiner,

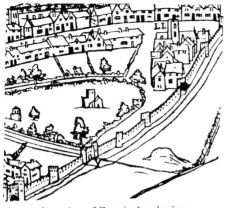

A section of Cunningham's view
of Norwich in 1558 showing
St Catherine's church and its 'plain'.

builder and wheelwright. Adam Hyslop was a tea dealer and draper of the travelling kind, Charles Crowe an upholsterer (and paper-hanger), and there was a private resident listed by the name of Mrs Beaumont. There were also three hostelries on St Catherine's Plain: the Black Horse, kept by George Hammond, the London Steam Packet by Isaac Hartt, and the Rose Tavern kept by William Wordingham again.

The plain recalls one of the lost churches of Norwich. It was situated within the triangle of land bounded by All Saints Green, Surrey Street and Queen's Road, close to the point where these last two roads merged.

The eighteenth century historian Francis Blomefield said that the church 'was first dedicated to St Winewaloci or Winewaloy, commonly called Winall who was bishop and confessor and had 3rd March kept holy to him; at the time of Norwich Domesday it appears to have been rededicated to St Catherine'.

The rededication may, however, have come later, but King Stephen gave the church to the nuns of Carrow Priory. The priory, founded around 1146, was a Benedictine nunnery which boasted the largest Norman church in Norwich after the Cathedral. Remains of it can still be seen on land which once belonged to the Colmans within the environs of their factory site.

In 1349, the Black Death reached these shores, a dreadful pestilence which killed one in three of the population, devastating whole communities. Blomefield said that the parish of St Catherine's 'was almost depopulated by the great pestilence, and never recovered since but dwindled away.' The church fell into disrepair and was eventually demolished. But its name lives on in the plain and also in the fine Georgian house known as St Catherine's Close which houses the BBC on All Saints Green.

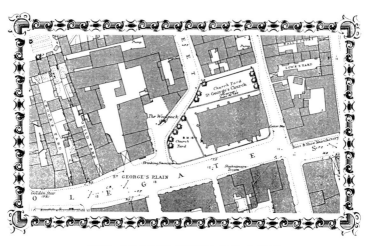

ST GEORGE'S PLAIN

Kelly's Directory for 1968 gave this plain a separate identity within Colegate (charcoal gate). It was the address of Howlett and White Ltd., shoe manufacturers, and the Norvic Shoe Co.Ltd., as well as the name of a bus stop outside the factory entrance. Across the road was Howlett and White, leather merchants, occupying the building which now houses Radio Broadland.

No sign marks St George's Plain but the name is still applied to this length of Colegate. It is Radio Broadland's address. A large if rather weathered board, standing on Duke Street, sets out the phases of redevelopment which have taken place to the old shoe factory by Norwich Property Investments Group. Beneath a logo depicting the saint, the words St George's Plain stand out in bold lettering.

The plain begins in the triangular area where Muspole Street enters Colegate, and runs the entire length of the shoe factory. (*Kelly's Directory* breaks the entry with a short rule to indicate that St George's Plain ends after the Norvic Shoe Factory).

'St George's-in-Colegate,' wrote Arthur Mee in 1951, 'is among the shoe factories. Once its companions were the houses of the rich, but the church itself is now a fine place with a forsaken air.'

Some of the rich companions have survived such as Bacon House just east of the church on the corner of St George's Street and Colegate. This fine, timber-framed building, with a ground floor wall of flint, was built for Henry Bacon, a wealthy worsted merchant who was Sheriff of Norwich in 1548 and Mayor in 1557 and 1566. The house was probably built to mark his year as Sheriff but archaeologists have suggested that part of it was constructed a decade earlier, during the 1530s. The west wing is certainly older, dating from the previous century.

One of the city's official green plaques fixed to the wall commemorates Bacon and also informs us that the house had associations with Kett's Rebellion in 1549. When Thomas Codd, who was Mayor of the city, became a prisoner of the rebels, he deputed Augustine Steward to act as Mayor on his behalf. Steward, so Nicholas Sotherton said, 'wyth Mr Harry Batto, Alderman, [actually Henry Bacon] and John Atkins, Shreives, wyth other theyr assistence kept the Cytezins, except the most vagrant and vacabond persons, in good quiet.' It is said that Bacon entertained the Earl of Warwick, commander of the second Royal army sent to put down the uprising, to dinner. Undoubtedly some of Warwick's officers were billeted in Bacon house. The Earl himself lodged with Augustine Steward on Tombland, while 'other Lords, Squires and Gentlemen the like and for the tyme took each man's howse as there owne till theyr departure .'

St George's Church, Colegate

The church of St George was founded in the late eleventh or early twelfth century and like other Norwich churches was extensively rebuilt in later centuries. The tower and nave were completed in 1459; the chancel in 1498; the north aisle, with the chapel of St Mary in 1505, and the south aisle, with St Peter's Chapel in 1513. This handsome Perpendicular church evokes the wealth of the merchants who lived around it and its fine Georgian furnishings reflect a period of prosperity in the eighteenth century.

The south aisle chapel is the final resting place of a man George Borrow described in *Lavengro* as 'the little dark man with the brown coat and the top-boots, whose name will one day be considered the chief ornament of the old town, and whose works will at no distant period rank amongst the proudest pictures of England - and England against the world! thy master, my brother, thy, at present, all too little considered master - Crome.'

John Crome died on 22nd April 1821, thirty years before *Lavengro* was published. Borrow had become acquainted with Crome when the artist came to their house in Willow Lane to give instruction to George's elder brother John. How prophetic those words turned out to be. Crome lies beside Mayors and Sheriffs of Norwich, men of substance, men of wealth well-known in their day; but it is the poor artist who is now remembered for the richness of his 'English pictures ...beautiful rural pieces, with trees which might well tempt the wild birds to perch upon them.' A monument marks the site of his earthly shell yet old Crome's spirit lives on in paint and canvas, the skill and brilliance of his work measured now in

John Crome

tens of thousands of pounds, and on view in galleries and private collections throughout the world. Like a subtitle, his name is linked to St George's, the board outside proudly proclaiming it as 'John Crome's Church.'

The neighbouring Woolpack public house, a pleasant Georgian building, occupies the site of a thirteenth century house which belonged to the Augustinian Priory of our Lady at Walsingham. Conveyed to John the Prior in 1298, it provided a comfortable and convenient town house for the Prior and the large retinue he usually brought with him when visiting the city. Most of the larger orders, with abbeys situated in the county, had such private houses in Norwich; they remained in use until the dissolution of the monasteries in the sixteenth century.

The Woolpack, once the townhouse of the Prior of Walsingham

In the official *Norwich Guide* (undated but published around thirty years ago), the late Eric Fowler, better known to readers of the *Eastern Daily Press* by his pseudonym Jonathan Mardle, wrote: 'St George's Plain is typical of the industrial district of "Norwich Over the Water." The whole district is now lamentably run down, but there are hopes that, as industry moves to the outskirts of the city, the old ward of "Over the Water" may be redeveloped with new houses and flats, and restored to life and use as a residential district.'

Hopes were transformed into reality. During the 1970s, an ambitious revitalisation scheme gradually turned a decaying, untidy, industry-scarred area of Norwich into a pleasant one, mixing older, refurbished buildings with tastefully designed new ones befitting a 'fine city.'

The Norvic shoe factory, once the largest of its kind under one roof in the country, is a testimony to what can be achieved with creative and sympathetic planning. Instead of demolishing it completely, the building underwent extensive alteration and restoration into shops, offices and flats. The façade now stands as a monument not only to Victorian architecture but also to a major industry which brought prosperity to the city and employment to thousands of its inhabitants.

31

From small beginnings in Swan Lane, the shoe manufacturers Tillyard and Howlett moved, during 1856, into a purpose-built factory on St George's Plain, designed by Robert Kitton. Throughout the nineteenth century the shoe trade expanded, and over the next sixty years the factory grew to cover the whole block between St George's Street in the east, Duke Street in the west, Colegate in the north and the river Wensum to the south.

George White (later to be knighted) became a partner in 1875, and the name of Tillyard was dropped. During the following year the grand façade consisting of seven bays was built by Edward Boardman. In 1894 he added another eight bays creating the impressive edifice which dominates the plain completely, almost dwarfing the church.

In 1911 the firm changed its name to the Norvic Shoe Co. Ltd., although Howlett and White still appeared in *Kelly's Directories* into the late 1960s. During the 1970s, however, the trade had gone into decline and the factory was forced to close in 1980.

The Norvic Shoe Factory, architect Edward Boardman

When Howlett and White changed the company's name to Norvic, it was recalling one of the older Latin names for Norwich. Coins struck during the reign of Aethelstan (AD 924-939) bear the mint signature 'Norvic'. These coins were minted in Northwic providing evidence of a settlement that had grown in importance over a thousand years ago. Mints could only be established in

32

defended 'burghs' and Northwic was one of four Saxon riverside settlements which merged to form the town of Norwich.

Archaeological evidence is beginning to suggest that a defended area existed to the north of the river Wensum with its centre running roughly along Magdalen Street. Traces of a tenth-century ditch and earth embankment, marking the settlement's western boundary, have been uncovered running north along the line of St George's Street. The Norvic shoe company had almost brought the name back to its very roots, missing the probable site of Northwic by only a few yards. Norvic remains to this day part of the signature of the Bishop of Norwich, preceded by his Christian name. And from the Latin stem also comes the word for a true born son or daughter of Norwich, Norvicensian.

Before St George's Plain came to be dominated so completely by Boardman's great factory, it appears to have been a mixture of residential and business premises. In the 1840s, the Woolpack was run by Mary Barnes who was also a coal merchant. Elizabeth Chambers ran a beer house and a grocery shop. There was a timber merchant, a yarn agent, a baker and a dyer and dresser. Joseph Stannard was an architect, land agent and surveyor and, with his brother Richard, built houses as well. Two academies or schools are listed on the plain, one of which took boarders.

The nineteenth century saw the gradual deterioration of Colegate from a street of gentlemen's residences to an industrial one. The expansion of Howlett and White's factory swept away houses, including, during the 1890s, the birthplace of Amelia Opie, only child of a prominent local physician, Dr James Alderson. A green plaque on the wall of the former shoe factory describes her briefly as an 'authoress and philanthropist'.

Born in 1769, she took over the running of her father's household at fifteen following the death of her mother. Many a young woman in similar circumstances would have remained dutifully tied to her father and died a spinster. Not Amelia. Beautiful and intelligent, she made an impact on Norwich Society attending balls, soirées and the theatre. Yet she was no mere frivolous socialite; there was a deeper side to her nature, which led to a lifelong study of the psychology of crime. She frequently attended trials at Norwich Assizes or in the London Courts, listening to the cases and studying the criminals. She became,

33

too, a familiar figure in London society where she often stayed as a guest at the home of the actress Sarah Siddons. Amongst her acquaintances were Mary Wollstonecraft, Richard Brinsley Sheridan, Lord Byron and William Wordsworth. From childhood she had written poems, ballads and plays; at 18 she played the heroine in a private production of her tragedy *Adelade*.

In 1794, she was introduced to John Opie, the fashionable portrait painter, who had only recently divorced his wife. Romance followed and four years later they married and settled in London. It was largely through his influence, persuading her to write seriously, that she produced her first successful novel, *Father And Daughter*. Despite the *Edinburgh Review* later calling it 'an appalling piece of domestic tragedy', by 1844 it had run to twelve editions. In 1807 John died and Amelia returned to Norwich to live with her father.

By this time she had become deeply interested in the Society of Friends whose meetings she had regularly attended from around 1814. Two months before the death of her father in 1825 she pronounced herself a Quaker. ('She is all Quakerized you know' Miss Mitford confided to a friend.) Joseph John Gurney of Earlham (described as the Quaker Pope) was a widower and Amelia may have had hopes of becoming the second Mrs Gurney, but it was not to be; when he did remarry it was to one of his cousins.

Amelia, however, maintained her Quaker beliefs, balancing the sobriety of behaviour and dress with the kind of social life she had always enjoyed. As Miss Sedgwick observed 'the fashionable little train to her pretty satin gown indicated how much easier it was to adopt a theory than to change one's habits.'

In 1832, she sold the house in Colegate and lived in Cornwall and Scotland for a time. She was 80 when she returned to Norwich where she took a house on Castle Meadow. Beside it ran a lane which in the eighteenth century was called Devil's Alley. It has since been widened and her house demolished. It was renamed Opie Street in her memory.

Amelia Opie died on 2nd December 1853, aged 84. She was buried in Norwich at the Friends Burial Ground in Gildencroft, beside the remains of her father. The site of her home in Castle Meadow is commemorated by a wall plaque and she by a statuette on top of a low building about halfway along the street that bears her name.

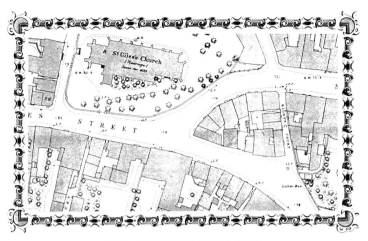

ST GILES' PLAIN

This is another of those plains which seem to live in the memory. There is no sign to mark it and *White's Directory* of 1845 does not list it in the streets section. But on tracing through the 'Classification of Trades and Professions', Jas. Cuddon and Son, conveyancers, are listed 'on St Giles' Plain'. As well as being an attorney, Cuddon appears to have been an insurance agent. Under the heading 'Fire and Life Offices', his firm acted for three companies - County, Eagle and Provident. Further on in the listing of Trades and Professions, a Milliner by the name of Emma de Vear, and a tailor, Charles Rogers, had their premises on St Giles' Plain.

Before Cleveland Road cut a swathe through the building line on the southern side, linking St Giles' Street with the Chapel Field Road/Grapes Hill bottleneck of a roundabout in the late 1960s, St Giles' Plain was a triangular open space where Bethel Street and St Giles' Street merged.

These two streets are a legacy of the Norman town, for in the years following the Conquest in 1066 the face of Norwich changed. The focus of town life and commerce was moved away from the old Saxon market of Tombland, to an area just west of the newly-constructed castle. What had probably been open fields or common land before the Conquest became the 'French Borough', the 'Franci de Norwic' in the Domesday Book of 1086. This borough took

35

General view of St Giles' Plain

shape around a large market where the present market is situated. Two streets left the market, both heading in a westerly direction: Lower Newport (St Giles' Street) and Upper Newport (Bethel Street).

They converge outside the church of St Giles which is reputed to have been founded during the reign of William the Conqueror (1066-1087) by Elwyn, a priest who subsequently gave it to the monks of Norwich Cathedral Priory. Because of its position on some of the highest ground within the city (about 85 feet above sea-level), it was often referred to as St Giles-on-the-Hill.

'It was wholly rebuilt in the reign of Richard II,' wrote William White, 'and is now one of the handsomest churches in Norwich.' Building and rebuilding went on over the centuries, but the nave with its splendid hammerbeam roof does date from the late fourteenth century when Richard was on the throne. The porch, decorated with a lovely fan-vaulted roof, is fifteenth century but the chancel is much later. The original was demolished in 1581 to save the Dean and Chapter of Norwich Cathedral, in whose patronage the church was, the expense of repairing it. It was rebuilt, along with the north vestry, in the nineteenth century.

At 120 feet the tower, surmounted by a wooden bell-cot, is the tallest of all the city's parish churches. Because of its dominant position on high ground, it was used as a beacon tower during Kett's Rebellion. The iron basket which contained the fire is still preserved inside the church. It was also a convenient position for soldiers stationed at Britannia Barracks (now Norwich Prison) on Mousehold to practise their semaphore signalling; the barracks are easily visible from the tower.

St Giles also possesses a monument that is something of a rarity, the only tablet in East Anglia carved by the hand of the eighteenth century London sculptor Sir Henry Cheere. It commemorates Thomas Churchman, an alderman of the city who died in 1742 aged 72. A prosperous worsted merchant and weaver, Thomas built himself a town house opposite the church during the 1720s. His son, also christened Thomas, Mayor in 1761 and later knighted by George III, enlarged the property around 1750, extending the frontage to create the impressive building we see today.

Churchman House has retained the name of the father and son who built it, although it subsequently passed through several worthy and distinguished hands. Notably, it was where Miss Ada Benson began the Norwich High School for Girls in February 1875. The school occupied the building for two years then moved to the Assembly House.

During the eighteenth and nineteenth centuries, St Giles' Street was virtually the Harley Street of Norwich. Several doctors had their homes and practices in some of the fine Georgian Houses, and after the school left Churchman House, Doctor Peter Eade purchased the property. Born in 1825 at Acle where his father was a doctor, Eade was physician to the Norfolk and Norwich Hospital from 1858 to 1888. Side by side with his medical career, he played a distinguished role in the civic life of the city as a councillor and magistrate. In 1880, he became Sheriff and later served three terms as Mayor in 1883, 1893 and 1895, the year in which he was honoured with the Freedom of the City. In respect of his public service, Queen Victoria conferred a knighthood on him in 1885.

A director of the Norwich Union Life Assurance Society, a trustee of the Norwich Savings Bank, a great advocate of open spaces within the city which led to the laying out of Chapel Field

37

Churchman House, first home of the Norwich High School
for girls

Gardens and the development of Mousehold Heath as a public place, Sir Peter was also an author, local historian and a committee member of the Norfolk and Norwich Archaeological Society. As well as writing on medical topics, he published a *History of the Parish of St Giles* and a *History of the Norfolk and Norwich Hospital.*

His busy life came to an end in 1915 when he had reached the grand old age of 90. His obituary in The Lancet described him as 'one of the best known provincial physicians in the country.' Despite his history of the parish and his presentation of a stained glass window to the church in 1904, Sir Peter was not buried there. His final resting place is in the churchyard of St Andrew and St Peter in Blofield.

Following the death of his wife Ellen less than a year later, Churchman House stood empty until it was purchased by Norwich Corporation in 1919. Even then the building retained a medical connection by becoming the offices for the city's health department. Around 1990, Churchman House underwent extensive restoration and is now the Norwich Register Office, providing a fine and elegant backdrop for civil marriage ceremonies.

In Sir Peter Eade's day, his immediate neighbour in Number 70 St Giles Street was another eminent physician at the Norfolk and Norwich Hospital, Sir Frederic Bateman who died in 1904 aged 80. His house, which was actually much older than the Georgian façade it presented to the world, was destroyed in an air raid on 27th June 1942 along with Number 72. This appears to have been a building of Tudor origin which had been altered and strengthened to create the furniture showroom of Walter Kett and Sons. Fortunately, Churchman House survived the blitz but Bateman's house was never replaced; the now redundant Gospel Hall occupied what was once a part of the garden. Kett's furniture store was rebuilt as a single-storey showroom but demolished in the 1960s to make way for a new road. Cleveland Road now cuts through the site of Bateman's home and Kett's shop.

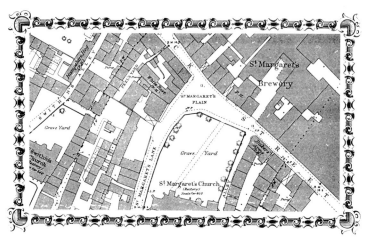

ST MARGARET'S PLAIN

Norwich has been rightly called a city of churches. On the eve of the Norman Conquest, the Saxon town, hugging the banks of the river Wensum and numbering around 5,500 inhabitants, had at least twenty-five churches. (The Domesday Book of 1086 implies that there could have been as many as forty churches and chapels).

Their number increased with the city's subsequent growth. By the early fourteenth century there were sixty-one parish churches within the walls. Four ceased to function as the Black Death of 1349-1350 took its toll of the population, killing around one in three. Some parishes were depopulated as has already been noted in St Catherine's Plain.

Changes in religious ideas, thoughtless town planning and movements in population as the city spread beyond its protective curtain of flint walls, reduced the number further. George Borrow in *Lavengro* wrote poetically of the city's 'thrice twelve churches,' while William White in 1845 stated that there were 'no fewer than 39 *parish churches*'.

Until the outbreak of World War II, thirty-six churches had managed to survive the vicissitudes of time. Heavy bombing reduced the number to thirty-one but still left Norwich with a unique legacy of more medieval churches than any other town. Many of them no longer function as places of worship and several have been put to secular use; all of them, however, have been maintained and can be visited.

St Benedict's Street provides a good illustration of just how densely populated the parishes were. Three churches stand within a few hundred yards of each other; even at the turn of the nineteenth and twentieth centuries the wedge-shaped district between Westwick Street and St Benedict's Street contained homes for around 1,100 people.

Moving from west to east, this trio of churches is composed of the small St Swithin, the middle-sized St Margaret's and the larger St Laurence. These parishes were probably founded before the Norman Conquest and the churches rebuilt in later centuries.

St Margaret's is in the Perpendicular style, consisting of a chancel, spacious nave, south aisle, north porch, south porch and embattled square tower. Much of the building dates from the fifteenth century but the tower shows workmanship of a century earlier with the belfry openings having decorated tracery. An image of St Margaret with a monk is carved in the spandrel of the south porch.

St Margaret's Church

The church suffered some years of neglect in the second half of the nineteenth century but repairs were carried out in 1869 and further restoration was undertaken in 1886. Damage caused by bombing in the last war was repaired between 1948 and 1951.

St Margaret's remained a place of worship until 1977 when

41

redundancy cast a shadow over its future. In 1981 it had ceased to provide for spiritual needs but catered for bodily needs instead when it became a gymnasium and health club. Now it is empty, apart from the occasional exhibition, and is under the care of the Historic Churches Trust. The north part of the churchyard contains a small playground for young children.

But what of St Margaret's Plain? Was it to the north or south of the church? There is no street sign to provide an official answer and reference to William White clouds the issue somewhat. In 1845, White listed four businesses and one private resident on the plain. His listing also implies that it was to the south as he links it with Upper Westwick Street as St Benedict's was then known. Westwick Street he called Lower Westwick. But St Margaret's Plain actually lies to the north in the square created by the churchyard. Before the war, Westwick Street used to widen slightly at this point until pre-war demolition and German bombs altered the northern side completely.

St Margaret's Churchyard

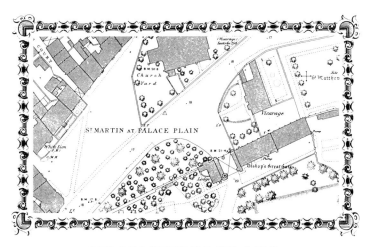

ST MARTIN'S PLAIN

Nicholas Sotherton writing in the 1550s described St Martin's as 'the playne before the Pallace gate'. Four centuries later, Eric Fowler said that it was 'one of the finest of the open squares - known locally as "plains" - in which Norwich abounds.'

The street sign calls it St Martin's Plain but it is often referred to as St Martin at Palace Plain or simply as Palace Plain. With its church, its fine group of houses, the sweep towards Whitefriars Bridge, all standing in the shadow of the Cathedral, this plain forms a delightful square, spoilt only by the volume of traffic which passes through it. Yet a master-stroke of Victorian planning sited the gasworks there in 1858. It may have provided the city 'with the benefits of a dependable gas supply' but fumes, smoke and smut drifted on to the Cathedral, the Close and much of the city centre. The river Wensum was polluted for quite a distance with residue from the production of gas. Construction of this eyesore in such an historic quarter of Norwich removed several old buildings including the surviving parts of Sir Thomas Erpingham's fifteenth century town house off World's End Lane. This quaintly-named thorough-fare was itself obliterated when the works were expanded in 1880.

Photographs well illustrate how dismal the area looked and it was not until 1970 that the gasworks were demolished. In recent years further work has been carried out to refurbish the plain but much of worth had already been lost; the destruction caused by the construction and subsequent expansion of the gasworks was thorough to say the least.

Archaeological excavations carried out by the adjacent riverside have given a fascinating glimpse into the area's Saxon past. Seeds found in soil samples taken in 1979 indicated that flax was soaked and then beaten to separate the fibres from the woody tissue. An eleventh century wickerwork fence was uncovered during an excavation in 1981. Such fences along the foreshore supported the sides of hard landing areas, created by the dumping of rubbish, animal dung and straw, on which boats could be beached for loading and unloading. These landing areas were only a short distance from the market place of Tombland. In those days there was no Cathedral or Close and Tombland was much more extensive than it is today.

Whitefriars Bridge derives its name from the friary of the Carmelites or White Friars which was established on the other side of the river in 1256. The site is now occupied by Jarrold's printing works. The river may have been bridged at this spot before the Norman invasion, but St Martin's Bridge, as the first wooden structure was called, had certainly been built by 1106.

The Earl of Warwick ordered the destruction of all bridges linking the southern and northern parts of the city in order to frustrate rebel attacks during Kett's uprising. Perhaps as a result of pressure from influential citizens who, like Henry Bacon, had their homes in the northern area Over-the-Water, the full plan was not carried out. Only one bridge suffered; in the words of Nicholas Sotherton 'the bridge callyd Whyt Fryars bridge was broken clene up'.

Until the sixteenth century, the bridge had always been made of wood. In 1591, according to William White 'it was rebuilt of stone, containing one pointed arch, 30 feet span, but being much decayed, it was thoroughly repaired in 1835, when the old battlements gave place to neat iron railing.'

In 1924, it was replaced by the present structure. While the old bridge was being dismantled, a great deal of care was taken to number each stone. Obviously the intention was to preserve as much as possible and re-erect it elsewhere. To this end, the stones were entrusted to Norwich Corporation for safekeeping and never seen again. When questions were eventually asked, the Corporation was forced to admit that the remains of Whitefriars Bridge had become hardcore during the construction of Aylsham Road.

Long before Herbert de Losinga's workmen began building his great Cathedral in 1096, a small church dedicated to St Martin had stood on the same piece of rising ground that the present church occupies. Perhaps it had already been there for a century when the Normans arrived. Even archaeologists cannot be completely sure of its foundation date. The only certainty is that two timber structures preceded the first stone church which was probably in place before 1066.

Consisting of a nave and chancel, it was one of a handful of Norwich churches actually mentioned by name in the Domesday Book. 'A certain church of St Martin is also in the Borough, which Stigand held before 1066.' Stigand was then Archbishop of Canterbury and enjoyed a considerable holding of land and property in the town, including some fifty houses. So it would appear that St Martin's was a church of some importance in Saxon Norwich.

The square tower and north aisle were added during the fourteenth century, the south aisle in the fifteenth century. Evidence does remain of pre-Conquest workmanship; on the exterior eastern wall of the chancel the corners consist of Saxon long-and-short work in Barnack limestone.

One interesting architectural feature is the insertion of three small quatrefoil clerestory windows on each side of the nave. These actually date from the second half of the nineteenth century and are a unique feature amongst the Norwich churches.

The upper part of the tower fell down in 1783 and was rebuilt without the top storey. Not until a century later was it restored to its original height. During restoration work in 1851, the north aisle and most of the chancel, except for the east end, collapsed, a catastrophe from which sixteen workman were lucky to escape unscathed. Bombing during the last war inflicted some damage, mainly to the stained glass which was later restored incorporating some of the original figures into the new windows.

Worship ceased there during the 1960s and a number of different schemes were proposed for its subsequent use. Following the completion of the new law courts, the decision was made to convert the old church into a day centre for the Probation Service. Before conversion work began, archaeologists were able to excavate the interior in 1988 and study the various building phases of the church's long history.

As two other churches in the city were also dedicated to the same saint, location came to form a part of their name. St Martin In Balliva stood at the southern end of the castle bailey, coming into the jurisdiction or bailiwick of the castle. Demolished in 1562, its site is marked by a green plaque on the wall of the offices of Eastern Counties Newspapers. St Martin at Oak, named because of an oak tree which once stood in its graveyard, still exists, used now as a night shelter for the homeless.

St Martin at Palace gained its identity from its proximity to the Bishop's Palace, now a part of the Norwich School. Just south of the church, across Bishopgate, is the splendid fifteenth century gateway leading to the former Palace. More like the entrance to a castle or walled city, the gateway has two arches: the larger for carriages, the smaller for pedestrians. William Alnwick, Bishop of Norwich from 1426 until 1436, was responsible for building the gate which was completed during the last year of his office at the Cathedral, before his translation to the See at Lincoln.

The Gateway to the Bishop's Palace

One of the more striking secular buildings on Palace Plain is the three-storey Georgian mansion which bears the name Cotman House. A stone plaque with his image in relief informs us that 'John Sell Cotman 1782 - 1842 One of the most famous of the Norwich School of Painters lived in this house.' He resided there for ten years, from 1824 until 1834, and opened on the premises a 'School for Drawing and Painting in Water Colours'. His terms were one and a half guineas a quarter but his income did not match a rather extravagant lifestyle and he was evicted.

Palace Plain, showing Cotman House in the centre

Next door stands the former White Lion public house. A photograph taken during the early 1980s shows the words 'Estbd. 1787' on the fascia sign. The building dates back to the sixteenth century and on its façade are carved two small shields each supported by the figure of an angel. In 1845, the historian Charles Muskett described the shields as 'quite plain, having neither arms nor date; their history cannot therefore be traced.' Arms were subsequently added, but whose? Those of the Blomefields according to one history of Norwich public houses. Other sources are more cautious and a question mark still hangs over these emblems.

When the law courts moved into Bishopgate, the name of the pub was changed to the Wig and Pen in deference to the legal profession. It is now a favourite lunchtime haunt of barristers and solicitors.

At the other end of this row of buildings is Number 10 St Martin's Plain, at present occupied by a dress shop. Set into its wall is a fine oriel window dating from the fifteenth century. Installed in 1970, it came from another building across the plain once connected with the name of Sir Thomas Erpingham. Some histories

Number 10, St Martin's Plain with its 'borrowed' window

of the city's public houses have stated that the 'Bee Hive' in Palace Plain was originally the home of Sir Thomas. Archaeologists working on the site during demolition in 1962 reached a different conclusion. 'The name of this house is misleading,' said the Bulletin of the Norfolk Research Committee, summarising their work for 1961 and 1962, 'for it is unlikely that it was ever part of Erpingham House, which was further along World's End Lane, and is more correctly named Calthorpe's House.' Substantial parts of Erpingham House had survived until 1858 but were destroyed to make way for the gasworks.

The repositioned window is still, on occasions, linked to Sir Thomas. The truth does, to some extent, destroy the romance for here was a man who should rank with Nelson as one of the county's and, indeed, the country's great heroes. Born in 1357 in the north Norfolk village from which his forebears took their name, Sir

Thomas served John of Gaunt and later Gaunt's son, Henry Bolingbroke. He fought, quite literally, all over Europe, in Scotland, Spain, France, and Italy and beside the feared Teutonic knights at Danzig, Königsburg and the siege of Vilna. He also served in Jerusalem and on the islands of Cyprus and Rhodes.

In the complex and volatile politics of late fourteenth century England, he certainly backed the right side. Richard II's reign from 1377 until 1399 was a twenty-two year struggle between the King (Edward III's grandson) and the family of Lancaster led by John of Gaunt (Edward's third son) and subsequently Bolingbroke. When Bolingbroke finally seized the throne in 1399 as Henry IV, Sir Thomas was one of the commissioners who received the surrender of Richard's crown. His loyal support of the House of Lancaster was rewarded with honours and estates. In 1400, he was made Warden of the Cinque Ports; Constable of Dover and Framlingham Castles, and a Knight of the Most Noble Order of the Garter. In 1404, he became Steward of the Royal Household and acting Marshal of England. During the same year his influence with the King helped gain Norwich another important Charter, which separated the city from the county and made Norwich a county in itself, with the power to elect a Mayor and two Sheriffs instead of bailiffs.

His finest hour came in the French campaign under Henry V when he commanded the English archers at Agincourt on 25th October 1415, a victory won in the face of tremendous odds. In thanksgiving for coming safely through the battle, Sir Thomas erected the magnificent gateway to the Cathedral which bears his name; his carved effigy kneeling in prayer can be seen in a niche directly above the lofty arch.

He married twice in his long and eventful life, first Joan Clopton who died in 1404 and secondly Joan Walton in 1409, sister and heir to John Walton of Wivenhoe and widow of Sir John Howard. She died in 1424. Sir Thomas lived on into his seventy-first year and after his death in 1428 his body was laid to rest in Norwich Cathedral.

His spirit lives on all too briefly in the pages of Shakespeare's *Henry V*. On the night before Agincourt the King is in conference with Bedford and Gloucester when they are interrupted by Sir Thomas. Henry immediately breaks off to greet him.

K. Henry	Good morrow, old Sir Thomas Erpingham:
	A good soft pillow for that good white head
	Were better than the churlish turf of France.

| Erpingham | Not so, my liege: this lodging likes me better, |
| | Since I may say 'Now lie I like a king.' |

As the night is chilly, the King borrows Sir Thomas's cloak so that he can walk around the camp.

| Erpingham | Shall I attend your grace? |

K. Henry	No, my good knight;
	Go with my brothers to my lords of England;
	I and my bosom must debate awhile,
	And then I would no other company.

| Erpingham | The Lord in heaven bless thee, noble |
| | Harry!   [Exit.] |

| K. Henry | God-a-mercy, old heart! thou speakest |
| | cheerfully. |

When the remains of Calthorpes house were excavated in 1962 by the Norfolk Research Committee, evidence that it dated back to the mid-twelfth century was discovered. Alterations had been made at varying stages in its history by the superimposition of new floors.

The name of Calthorpe now appears to be another erroneous link. Their house, like Erpingham's, stood elsewhere on the plain. St Martin's Church has a large altar tomb to Lady Elizabeth Calthorpe who died in 1758. The sides are decorated with coloured shields bearing coats of arms signifying her connection with leading local families, including that of Anne Boleyn. In the Cathedral is a tomb to Dame Elizabeth Calthorpe who was buried there in 1582.

The third name to be linked with this house is that of stone-mason Robert Everard who lived on Palace Plain during the fifteenth century. He was responsible for the beautiful stone vaulting of the Cathedral nave which replaced the old wooden roof badly damaged by fire in 1463 after the timber spire had been struck by lightning.

An adjoining house was occupied by another mason, John Antell. He also worked on the Cathedral and in three of Norwich's parish churches: St George Colegate, St Martin at Oak and St Michael Coslany.

In 1981, the old gasworks site gave up another of its secrets. While excavations were in progress before work began on the Magistrates' Court, the remains of a twelfth century building were uncovered. Dating from around the year 1170, it belonged to the Cathedral Priory as did all the land on which Palace Plain stands. Herbert de Losinga had acquired land in stages on which to build his great Cathedral and Benedictine Monastery. Although part of a grant of land made in 1106 ('from the bridge of St Martin to the land of St Michael'), the area of Palace Plain remained outside the actual precincts but in the ownership of the Priory.

The stone building served as a supply warehouse to the monastery because the tenants paid rent to the Cathedral cellarer. It appears to have been derelict by 1300 and may have been destroyed during the Tombland Riots of 1272. The surviving walls have been preserved inside a concrete cellar beneath the Magistrates' Court. Information panels outline the excavation and the main features of the building. The remains can be viewed by appointment with the Clerk to the Magistrates.

St Martin's Plain became a battlefield during Kett's Rebellion. On Thursday 1st August 1549, the Marquis of Northampton, who was in command of the first Royal army sent to Norwich to try and put down the uprising, placed a defensive line of troops and guns across the plain, blocking off the section where it merges with Bishopgate. He knew that from their camp on Mousehold the rebels would force their way past the isolated defences at Bishop's Bridge and make their way along Bishopgate. This they did, and attacked his line in great numbers head on. Other rebels, however, forced an entry through Pockthorpe Gate and, swarming over Whitefriars Bridge, hit Northampton's forces on the left flank. The fighting is said to have lasted three hours. In the course of the battle, Lord Sheffield, Northampton's second in command was thrown from his horse. Despite removing his helmet to reveal his identity and, as a Lord, buy his life with a reward, a carpenter by the name of Fulke clubbed him to death. A plaque in Bishopgate marks the spot where

51

Lord Sheffield died and he is buried beside other casualties of the fighting in St Martin's churchyard.

Shortly before noon, the defensive line collapsed. Lord Northampton's army was routed and fled in total disarray from the city. Norwich remained under rebel control until the Earl of Warwick arrived with a larger force on 24th August. Three days later Kett's men were defeated at Dussindale and the Norfolk Rebellion was over.

Before leaving St Martin at Palace Plain, it is worth mentioning one man who appears in *White's Directory* of 1845. He must have been something of a character in his day, and an enterprising one at that. Richard More first appears in the directory listings as a rag and bone merchant who also supplied manure. A page or two on, he is listed as a duffield and coarse woollen manufacturer with his own flock of sheep. No doubt his animals supplied the manure as well as the wool.

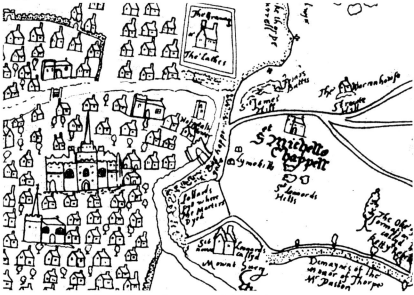

A section of a map of 1589 (redrawn)

It is possible to pick out the Castle and Cathedral, St Martin's church and the Bishop's Bridge over the Wensum, the Lollard's Pit and the remains of St Leonard's Priory which was occupied by Kett during the rebellion.

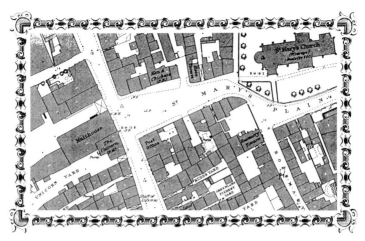

ST MARY'S PLAIN

Forming a link between Oak Street and Duke Street, St Mary's Plain, like Bank Plain, is a complete thoroughfare. With St Mary's Church, St Mary's Baptist Church, the Zoar Strict and Particular Baptist Chapel and a large publisher of hymn and religious books, it could be described as the religious centre of Norwich.

Like so much of the old ward Over-the-Water, slums and industry once stood side by side. In the last decade of the nineteenth century, St Mary's was surrounded by a 'region of noxious courts and alleys.' Tenements crowded in on the narrow streets which were liberally dotted with factories, breweries and malthouses. In 1920, old slum dwellings were pulled down to build St Mary's Works for the shoe manufacturers Sexton, Son and Everard. The factory still stands, occupied at present by the religious publishers Hymns Ancient and Modern. Opposite, along the southern side, council housing has replaced the old slum buildings.

Coslany, the word added to St Mary's to describe its location, was one of the four Saxon settlements which grew along the banks of the river Wensum to form the town of Norwich. South of the river were Westwic and Conesford, and to the north Northwic (although its position north or south of the river is still open to debate) and Coslany, an island, or an island in a bog. Over the centuries, perhaps through infilling, the island became part of the

53

north bank. A reference from the thirteenth century indicates two bridges at Coslany or a bridge in two parts ('duos pontes de Koselayne').

The area is quite low-lying and has often suffered from flooding especially between the sixteenth and nineteenth centuries. One such inundation in 1762 flooded the church to a depth of three feet, destroying a number of valuable old books and manuscript documents.

'A fine round tower with big belfry windows, built by the Saxons and restored in our time, rises at the west end of St Mary-at-Coslany, a cross-shaped church on a green island site,' was Arthur Mee's description in *The King's England*. It is the double belfry opening with round recessed shafts that betray its Saxon origins. Dating from the eleventh century and before the Conquest of 1066, it is considered to be the oldest church tower in Norwich.

St Mary's Church and Hymns Ancient and Modern in an old shoe-factory beyond.

In 1477, the main body of the church - nave, transepts and chancel - was rebuilt against the old tower. Restoration took place between 1857 and 1869 but within thirty years, like the surrounding slums, St Mary's had fallen into 'extreme dilapidation.' The annual report of the Norfolk and Norwich Archaeological Society in 1898 said that it was 'sad to see the state of ruin into which this fine building had been allowed to fall'. The roof was so bad that if rain happened to fall during a service, the members of the congregation were forced to resort to their umbrellas to keep themselves dry inside the building! How often this actually happened is hard to say because services had become infrequent.

Hopes were expressed that St Mary's would be restored. It was little more than a rubbish dump and a ready target for vandals, 'the stone-throwing street urchins.' By 1904, sections of the tower had fallen down and it seemed as if restoration would be impossible. The impossible was achieved, however. Rebuilding took place in 1908. The interior was refurbished and new windows installed. The damaged parts of the tower were repaired but it was never restored to its full height. It remains shorter by several feet, a difference that can be seen by comparing photographs taken in 1900 with later ones.

Fire bombs badly damaged the roof during an air raid in 1942 necessitating yet another restoration. Services began again in 1950 but its days as a place of worship were numbered. Like many of the city's parishes, the population had been declining steadily throughout the century as people moved from the centre to the outskirts. This, combined with a general decline in attendance, ensured that there were just too many churches serving too few interested people.

St Mary's became redundant in 1974 and new uses were sought for it. Plans to open it as a small theatre called the 'Luke Hansard Playhouse' fell through in 1979 because of lack of support. For financial reasons, the 'Friends of the Norwich Churches', who had set up their headquarters there, hoping that it would become a venue for exhibitions, concerts and meetings, were forced to abandon the scheme in 1983 after only two years. A useful new life began in 1985 when it opened as an antiques, arts and crafts centre which it has continued to be ever since.

Arts and crafts are arguably the most appropriate use to which this fine old church could be put, not only because Saxon and medieval craftsmen built it, but also through its connection with two of Norwich's finest artists. John Sell Cotman was baptized there in 1782, and ten years later it was the scene of John Crome's marriage to Phoebe Berney.

Cotman and Crome have left their names to posterity through the genius of their canvasses, but another man, a true craftsman in his own field, bore a name which was to enter the language as a word in its own right - Hansard, the official verbatim reports of proceedings in Parliament.

Luke Hansard was born in the parish and baptized in St Mary's Church during July 1752. Trained in Norwich as a printer, he settled in London in 1769, finding employment with the firm of John Hughs, printers to the House of Commons. Through skill and hard work, he rose quickly through the firm and, when Henry Hughs, the founder's son, retired, 48-year-old Luke became the sole proprietor in 1800. He was already a familiar figure in the corridors of Parliament, renowned for his care and diligence. Together with his sons Luke Graves and James, the firm expanded, and when he died on 29th October 1828, in his seventy-sixth year, he had amassed a fortune. The little man from Norwich who, as a child had never been 'nursed in the lap of luxury', who had arrived in London fifty-nine years before with only a guinea in his pocket, died worth £80,000.

That it is Luke's name which has become the Hansard of Parliamentary reportage is a popular misconception even, on occasions, in dictionaries. He was highly respected amongst all members of the House and he did a considerable amount of Government and other official printing, but never the verbatim accounts of the debates. This was the work of his oldest son Thomas Curson Hansard who left his father's firm in 1803 to set up on his own. His son, also called Thomas Curson, carried on the work, building from humble beginnings an aspect of Parliamentary printing that became synonymous with his family's name. Luke was merely the founder of a dynasty of Parliamentary printers.

By a remarkable coincidence, when the headquarters of Her Majesty's Stationery Office, which had produced Hansard since 1920, was moved from London to its present site on the corner of Duke Street and St Crispin's Road, it was only a few hundred yards from St Mary's where Luke had been baptized more than two centuries before. Hansard, in a way, had returned to its roots, to the city where a 14-year-old apprentice printer had first set a line of type.

St Mary's churchyard was once the largest in Norwich; despite losing part of its southern side it remains quite spacious. Surrounded by railings, it made a perfect grassy enclosure amidst the crowded houses and narrow streets. It is not surprising that in a bygone age country drovers used it as an overnight pen for their flocks and herds while attending the markets and fairs held in the city.

Redundancy may have overtaken the old medieval church, but opposite, on the southern side of the plain, St Mary's Baptist Church can have no such fears. Baptists have worshipped on this site for over 250 years interrupted only by the destructive effects of fire and world war.

The earliest meeting-house, utilising existing buildings of flint and brick, was opened in 1745. Sixty-seven years later, it was replaced as William White said 'in a more handsome manner.' Designed by Norwich architect Francis Stone, the new church had, in the words of one contemporary, an 'imposing front of white bricks, with Grecian portico on an ample flight of stone steps - altogether both within and without one of the handsomest Baptist meeting houses in the kingdom.'

One of its most notable features was the plaster ceiling shaped like a groined vault which skilfully and artistically hid the network of beams needed to support such a broad roof. The church was enlarged in 1839 at a cost of £1,000 and again in 1886 when an apse was added behind the pulpit for an organ and choir gallery.

On the morning of Sunday 10th September 1939, the church was damaged by fire. Restoration took just over a year and St Mary's reopened on Sunday 22nd September 1940. Within two years, however, it had been gutted following an air raid in the early hours of Saturday 27th June 1942. As a temporary measure, the congregation hired Stuart Hall where they worshipped for eight years until moving to the school in Duke Street. Application to rebuild was granted in October 1950 and the foundation stone laid by the Reverend Gilbert Laws on 5th July 1951.

The delicate problem of disturbing several graves to make way for the foundations was overcome by the creation of a new vault beneath the forecourt. The site is now marked by a cross cut into one of the paving slabs outside the main entrance.

Stanley J. Wearing, the architect responsible for the previous restoration, designed the new church to roughly the same dimensions as the old one. Inside, he created a sense of spaciousness by dispensing with the idea of supporting pillars and

57

spanning the entire width with a polygonal barrel vault. Eight pairs of windows assist in making the interior commendably light and airy.

Pykerell's House, saved from destruction

The church is bounded on its western side by Rosemary Lane which links St Mary's Plain via St Miles' Steps to the pleasant square surrounding St Michael's (or St Miles') Church on Colegate. Once a narrow little thoroughfare with houses crowding along either side, Rosemary Lane has changed completely during this century. A photograph taken around 1900 shows that had this lane survived the slum clearances and German bombs, it could have been transformed into a quaint and picturesque lane. Scarcely any of the original dwellings remain and Pykerell's House on the corner of Rosemary Lane and St Mary's Plain has been lucky to survive at all.

The removal of slum dwellings in the 1930s and German fire bombs in the 1940s have both threatened to obliterate this fine fifteenth century thatched house. It bears the name of Thomas Pykerell, a wealthy cloth merchant who was Sheriff of Norwich in 1513 and Mayor in 1525, 1533 and 1538. A rather weather-worn lead plaque also explains that it was once a 'Pilgrim's Hall' and latterly the 'Old Rosemary Tavern.'

The Norfolk Archaeological Trust purchased it during the 1930s, thus saving it from being reduced to a pile of rubble under the slum clearance scheme. But on 2nd August 1942, incendiary bombs set light to the roof causing a great deal of damage. Six years later it was fully restored and let once more to tenants. For lovers of heritage surely a most enviable place to live.

Although not officially a part of the plain but just to the east of St Mary's Church on the other side of Duke Street, is a splendid range of fifteenth and sixteenth century cottages. Once threatened with demolition, they were restored in the 1970s; unsympathetic additions were stripped away, and timbers exposed. An opening leads into Potter House Court, a picturesque courtyard which in summer is ablaze with flowers. Life has certainly returned to an area which, only twenty years ago, was untidy and run-down. Beneath the decay, underneath the layers of brick and plaster that had been slapped on to these buildings over the centuries, lurked their true historic character, a hidden beauty just waiting to be freed.

Restored buildings to the east of St Mary's Church

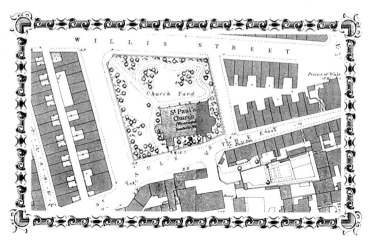

ST PAUL'S PLAIN

Children now play in a small garden that was once the corner of a churchyard. Two rows of terrace houses at right angles to each other are all that remain of the square which surrounded the small, round-towered church of St Paul. Most maps and directories called it St Paul's Square but William White writing in 1845 referred to it as 'the square called St Paul's plain.'

World war and town planning have destroyed both the church and its plain, leaving only a fragment of what was described in 1919 as the 'most picturesque square in the whole city at that time.'

Frederick Thurlow Hibgame wrote those words for an article entitled 'Recollections of Norwich Fifty Years Ago.' He went on to say that St Paul's 'showed a complete square of singularly quaint half-timbered houses. It looked very much then no doubt as it did in medieval times; but alas the jerry builder came along, down came all the old houses, and in their place arose dozens of hideous red-brick cottages, all exactly like one another, without a single thing to redeem their innate ugliness.'

Was it really quite so picturesque? A later edition of White's Directory published in 1883 presented a very different view. 'A rookery of disgraceful tenements in St Paul's has been demolished under the Artizan's Dwellings Act, and a colony of trim cottages erected in their place. The improvement cost the city £10,000.'

This view was shared by the eminent Norwich author, R.H.Mottram. In his book *If Stones Could Speak* he said that St Paul's Square was rebuilt by special Act of Parliament in the 1860s because the area had become 'dilapidated, verminous, disgraceful.'

Today scarcely anything is left. A truncated street bearing the name St Paul's Square remains of the western side, while Willis Street, now a cul-de-sac, marks the northern edge.

Road 'improvements' obliterated everything else. The inner ring road, like an ugly scar, cuts right across the old ward Over-the-Water; a stark soulless flyover, its drab concrete legs defacing historic Magdalen Street, takes the dual carriageway over Stump Cross and down to the Barrack Street roundabout where St Paul's church, surrounded by its plain, once stood. And yet it was a route chosen in the face of a much more sympathetic alternative.

In February 1931, Robert Atkinson, a Fellow of the Royal Institute of British Architects, suggested the alternative during a talk given to the Norwich Publicity Association. He said that there was 'a road to hand, ready made, the finest possible, and affording an opportunity that is unique. I refer to the old wall enclosing the city. On that wall, in almost every position, are slum dwellings put up during the last fifty years. It would be a great adventure to clear them all out and open up the road, following the wall which has always been a natural highway. Do this, and you will have a wonderful circulatory boulevard all round the city and its cost would be comparatively nothing.'

A Town Planning Report placed before the Council in 1936 advocated the present route cutting across the northern sector of the old city. This was even opposed in the 'City of Norwich Plan 1945' which outlined the ambitious plans for rebuilding the city after the war.

'*We are of the opinion,*' said the authors, '*that to cut through from Barrack Street west to Stump Cross and City Station, as then proposed, would make future congestion worse than that existing on all roads leading into the City from the north.*' They felt sufficiently strongly about this route to have the statement set in italics.

In the early 1970s the inner ring road was pushed through. The importance placed on the motor car created a road to the detriment of our heritage - a road, moreover, which is unlikely ever

61

to be completed as the planners originally envisaged. Yet the bottlenecks remain; those widened, improved roads still become choked with cars and trucks, and the attendant pollution damages not only the fabric of our buildings but the fabric of human lungs as well. In a way, the wheel has gone full circle. In many places Councils are seeking ways to discourage vehicles from entering towns and cities. It is, however, too late - in the case of Norwich and St Paul's Plain, thirty years too late.

St Paul's itself was a small church with a low round tower. W. H. Claxton in *Records of Local Events in Norwich, From 575 to 1904* gave its date of building as 'circa 1450.' It was probably around that time that the nave, north aisle and south porch were rebuilt against the old tower which contained Norman work in its lower part.

**St Paul's Church in the 1920s, now the site of the
Barrack Street roundabout**

A church had occupied the site for at least three centuries when the rebuilding took place. It had served not only the parish but also a monastic hospital for the poor and needy which had been established nearby during the first half of the twelfth century. Herbert de Losinga founded the hospital possibly only a year or two

62

before his death in July 1119, for work on the institution was completed by his successor, Eborard de Montgomery, Bishop of Norwich from 1121 until 1146.

St Paul's Hospital became known as Norman's Hospital probably deriving the name from one of its masters. Situated a short distance to the south of the church, it covered quite a large area and the extent of its site is marked on some of the older city maps.

Its function changed after the Dissolution. During the ten years from 1538 until 1548, all the monastic institutions within Norwich were dissolved. Only the Cathedral and Great Hospital remained largely intact; the City Corporation managed to retain several of the monastic hospitals utilising the buildings as poor-houses or for the isolation of plague victims. Norman's Hospital became the bridewell and was certainly being used as such in 1571. By 1583, however, the inmates had been moved to premises in St Andrew's, once the house of a wealthy merchant and first Mayor of Norwich, William Appleyard. His house has been known as the bridewell ever since and today is the Bridewell Museum.

Nothing now remains of Norman's Hospital; all the remnants, observed during the 1930s, of walls or reused building materials were swept away when the new road was constructed in 1970.

St Paul's Church survived intact into the present century. There were periods of neglect recorded in the eighteenth century. In 1773, notary William Utten observed that the interior walls were green and filthy, rain leaked into the vestry and one of the paths was completely overgrown with weeds. The situation had not improved five years later when he noted how bad the tower was and that the churchyard walls were falling down.

Improvements were carried out in the following century. The upper, octagonal part of the tower, was taken down and, according to William White, 'was rebuilt about 1819 of white brick, with stone coping.' Further work took place in 1870 when the chancel was added.

In 1882, the churchyard was laid out as a garden at the expense of John Gurney of Sprowston Hall. The interior was again renovated in 1921. A photograph taken about that time shows a pleasant little church surrounded by railings, its churchyard lush with trees and bushes, ivy creeping above the arch of its southern door.

Sadly, St Paul's was destroyed by incendiaries during the early hours of 27th June 1942. For ten years it stood a roofless ruin until the remains were demolished - demolished, moreover, despite all representations that the ancient round tower should, like St Benedict's, be allowed to remain.

The corner of St Paul's churchyard - now a children's playground

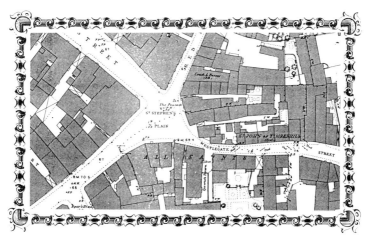

ST STEPHEN'S PLAIN

Today there is a busy road junction where St Stephen's Street, Rampant Horse Street, Red Lion Street and Westlegate meet. No street sign gives St Stephen's Plain formal recognition and its use has largely died out in recent years. Thirty years ago, *Kelly's Directories* were still giving the plain a separate identity. In the 1967 edition, for example, three businesses were listed on St Stephen's Plain: the Ipswich Tavern; Sexton Bros., fruiterers, and Dorothy Perkins Ltd., ladies' outfitters.

Comparing the present plain with photographs taken during the last two decades of the nineteenth century, the area has changed beyond all recognition. Planners, the trams and the Luftwaffe together share responsibility for the changes.

A photograph taken around 1895 shows a triangular shaped plain where the narrow streets all merged. No doubt its appearance had changed little in the fifty years since William White in his 1845 Directory had described the plain as having two inns: the City of Norwich and the Peacock; four other businesses, and the private residence of Allan Miller Thompson MD whose medical practice was nearby in Little Orford Street.

Changes started to take place in 1900. Old buildings along Red Lion Street were demolished so that the road could be widened for trams. New premises designed by George Skipper and Edward Boardman replaced the old. Twelve years later, Buntings new department store arose on the corner of St Stephen's Plain, which for generations afterwards would be known as 'Bunting's Corner'; to some amongst the older generation it still is.

St Stephen's Plain c. 1890

The business had occupied premises on the corner of Rampant Horse Street and St Stephen's Street since Arthur Bunting opened his Drapery and Furnishing store in 1866. The firm's slogan soon became 'Latest, Cheapest, and Best' priding itself on offering quality products at reasonable prices. By the first decade of this century, Buntings was offering a selection of items from Liberty's store in London at affordable prices.

In 1912, the old warren of eighteenth century buildings were replaced with a brand new purpose-built store, designed by Norwich architect Augustus Frederick Scott (1854-1936), a pioneer in the use of reinforced concrete. The style was neo-classical 'Adam' revival, inspired by the ideas of the great eighteenth century architect Robert Adam. Columns along the façade and a dome were features copied from contemporary London department stores, only on a smaller scale. However, in his use of stone and a reinforced concrete skeleton, Scott was able to construct a remarkably strong building even though the outside has a delicate look about it. The skeletal strength enabled him to create wide open, factory-like floors, giving a light and airy atmosphere with a maximum of display space. Such was the strength and the fireproof nature of the materials used that when the area was devastated by bombs, in April 1942, the building largely withstood the storm of fire and explosives. It lost its dome, suffered damage both inside and out but most of its form remained intact so that even today Scott's work can be appreciated in the building which now houses Marks and Spencer.

Following the air raids of 1942, Buntings moved into new premises in London Street where they were eventually taken over by Garlands.

Despite the changes to Red Lion Street and the construction of Buntings store, St Stephen's Street remained a narrow and very congested road throughout the first half of this century. In 1915, the City Council was offered the substantial sum of £10,000 towards widening the street by the directors of Great Eastern Railway, who wanted a much grander approach to their terminus at Victoria Station, an echo of the scheme of a century earlier which led to the creation of Prince of Wales Road as an approach to Thorpe Station. (In those days, Norwich could boast three railway stations: Thorpe, City and Victoria. Victoria was situated on Queens Road, its site now occupied by Sainsbury's which is why the design of the supermarket has something of the feel of a Victorian railway station about it.) Norwich Council refused the offer and in 1916 the Great Eastern Company turned Victoria Station into a goods yard with all passenger services using Thorpe Station.

As road traffic increased, discussions about widening St Stephen's continued throughout the 1930s, but agreement could not be reached on which side of the street should be demolished. The second world war helped precipitate some of the changes. As R. H. Mottram said in *If Stones Could Speak* (1953): 'Intensive bombing in 1942 has let a little daylight in, but, as has been pointed out, St Stephen's is so ridiculously incapable of carrying modern transport that it is a one-way street. It leads to precisely nothing.'

A year after those words appeared in print, work began to transform St Stephen's into the modern, spacious shopping street that the planners had long envisaged. St Stephen's Plain has become a busy cross roads, a bottleneck of vehicles and pedestrians. Traffic lights control the movements of people, cars, lorries and buses where, around thirty years ago, a policeman stood on a black and white striped podium like a conductor leading an orchestra, his well rehearsed hand-signals bringing a semblance of order to what might have been chaos.

St Stephen's Plain today, from Westlegate

St Stephen's in Cunningham's map of 1558

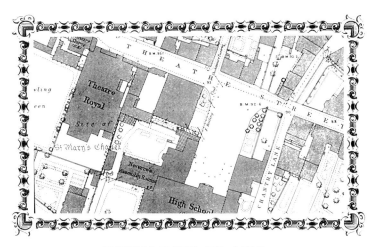

THEATRE PLAIN

Where Rampant Horse Street ends and Theatre Street begins (Church Lane, now renamed William Booth Street, running beside C & A's store to the top of Hay Hill marks the boundary) was once a narrow thoroughfare. Two cars could not pass and a photograph taken in 1965 reminds those of us who can remember, that the flow of vehicles along this narrow stretch was controlled by traffic signals. The street widened outside the Assembly House into Theatre Plain which is marked on A. W. Morant's map of 1873 as the forecourt of the Assembly House.

White's Directory of 1845 did not give the plain a separate entry in the streets section but called it Theatre Square. Later, however, in the Classification of Trades and Professions, he listed the address of J. and C. Cudbard, agricultural machine makers, as Theatre Plain.

Kelly's Directory (1937) does list the plain which was then the address of the Young Women's Christian Association, Norwich branch. The banana importers (as they were then described) E. Pordage & Co., in an advertisement in the same directory, gave their address as Theatre Plain.

Tracing down the Theatre Street entry in *Kelly's Directory*, the plain came after the Chantry and in its general description of Norwich the publication stated that the Theatre Royal 'stands a short distance from Theatre Plain.'

John Bracking in his article 'The Assembly House', published in *The Book of the Norwich Festival* to mark the Festival of Britain in 1951, said:

'*Norwich will proudly exhibit during the 1951 Festival fortnight - and let us hope for a long time afterwards - an architectural gem which escaped violent destruction almost by a miracle.*

This is the lovely Assembly House, Theatre Plain. A careful and thorough restoration has now brought this fine example of eighteenth-century good taste back into precisely the use for which it was built, though serving a far wider section of the community than ever it did during its Georgian heyday.'

From that time onwards it has been extensively used as a meeting place for clubs and societies, as a venue for art exhibitions, lectures, musical recitals and whist drives. The pleasant tea room and restaurant has become a favourite spot for locals and visitors alike to quench their thirst or satisfy their appetite in elegant surroundings. And in one of the wings was an intimate little cinema, the Noverre, which sadly closed in 1992 with plans for it to become a conference centre.

Even the fire of Wednesday 12th April 1995, which destroyed the roof and damaged the historic rooms with flame, smoke and water, proved to be only a temporary setback. Good arose from disaster as, under the supervision of experts from EnglishHeritage, the rooms were restored. Work on the décor, which might never otherwise have been carried out, brought about a spectacular transformation. Within two years, its doors were again open to the public.

Five centuries before the Assembly House was built, the College of St Mary in the Fields had been established on the site by John le Brun around the year 1250. Originally it was a hospital but soon 'became a noble College, consisting of a dean, (the founder being the first,) a chancellor, precentor, treasurer, and seven other prebendaries, with six chantry priests. The premises were extensive.' (William White 1845.) There was a church complete with a cloister and several buildings. The church's foundations were unearthed in 1901 during excavations to the Assembly House forecourt.

Following the Dissolution of the Monasteries, the community of priests was dispersed in 1544. The last Dean of the College,

70

The Assembly House

Its forecourt covers the foundations of the Church of St Mary in the Fields

Miles Spencer, bought the property cheaply from Henry VIII's commissioners, by persuading the other redundant priests to accept smaller pensions!

The church was demolished and, after Spencer's death in 1569, the property was bequeathed to his nephew, William Yaxley, who sold it to Sir Thomas Cornwallis of Brome in Suffolk. In 1573, Sir Thomas started to convert the remaining buildings into a town house. A new hall was constructed, a kitchen, gallery and porter's lodge built, the stables enlarged, a tennis court created and a garden laid out. Work was completed in 1586. Twenty-three years later the property was purchased by Sir Henry Hobart who later (1616) acquired Blickling Hall near Aylsham. It was one of the largest town houses in Norwich, second only in size to the Duke of Norfolk's Palace in St Andrew's.

In 1753, the property again changed hands, this time with the purpose of erecting a new building which would 'serve as a public place of entertainment for County and City.' The architect was Thomas Ivory (1709 - 1779) who actually worked to a plan by Sir James Burrough, Master of Gonville and Caius College in Cambridge, one of the best and most gifted amateur architects of his day.

Ivory remodelled the centre part of the mansion between its existing wings to create the Assembly House we see today. After completion in 1754, it became the 'in' place for the gentry of the time where 'tea, wine and cards' could be enjoyed at five shillings a head. According to William White it had 'a vestibule, two card rooms, a tea room, and two ball rooms, one 66 feet by 23, and the other 50 by 27. Between the ball rooms is the tea room, 27 feet square, separated from them by doors that are easily removed, so as to form one apartment 143 feet long.'

The entire length of this one apartment was 'illuminated by 10 branches holding 150 candles, and the company forming itself into one row may dance the whole length of the building, and then is presented such a scene of beauty and splendour as has few equals.' (Stacey's *History of Norfolk* 1818.)

Closure came in 1856. It was then bought for the use of the Norwich Freemasons by Benjamin Bond Cabbell who was Provincial Grand Master for the Order from 1854 until 1875. A. W. Morant's map of 1873 marks it as the Masonic Hall. By 1876, the Masons had decided to leave the Assembly House, wishing to find premises which could be made more adaptable to their own use. Three years later the fraternity moved into its present premises in St Giles Street.

For around fifty-six years, the Assembly House was occupied by the Norwich High School for Girls. The school moved out in 1933 and the building was left empty. Fortunate to escape demolition, it was used for several years as a warehouse until the Second World War when it became the headquarters of the Army Camouflage Unit. Despite heavy bombing which destroyed most of Orford Place and reduced nearby Caley Mackintosh's factory to a pile of rubble, the Assembly House came through unscathed.

The authors of the *City of Norwich Plan 1945* suggested that 'the Assembly Rooms in Theatre Street should be brought back into the life of the City.' Such schemes so often need a generous benefactor, and the old Assembly House found one in Henry Sexton, a wealthy shoe manufacturer. Shortly after the war, he purchased the property; S. Rowland Pierce FRIBA who, with C. H. James had designed the City Hall during the 1930s, was given the task of planning the restoration. In 1950, the Assembly House opened its doors to the public under the care of a trust. The whole project had cost Mr Sexton £70,000 but what a wonderful legacy he has left the city.

Less than fours years after the Assembly House had first opened to fashionable Georgian society, another of Thomas Ivory's projects was nearing completion on a neighbouring site. In *Records of Local Events in Norwich, From 574 to 1904*, W. H. Claxton gave a brief account of its opening: '1758. Jan 31. New Theatre opened with the comedy called *The Way of the World*, it stood at the corner of Theatre Plain.'

Ivory's design was highly regarded. One contemporary report said that it was 'the most perfect and compleat Structure of the kind in the Kingdom.' About a year after opening, it was being referred to as the 'Grand New Concert Hall'. Although theatrical productions were staged, the name was changed to the Theatre Royal in 1768 when it was licensed as a theatre by His Majesty's Letters Patent.

At the turn of the eighteenth and nineteenth centuries, various alterations and improvements were carried out. The proprietor, William Wilkins, built a colonnade on the front of the building, added a scene room and redecorated the interior. By 1819, however, plans were being drawn up for a new theatre to replace the original.

Wilkins' son, also called William, was the architect who designed and built the Shirehall in 1822 which stands at the foot of the Castle Mound and is now the home of the Royal Norfolk Regimental Museum. Having succeeded his father as proprietor of the theatre, he proceeded to demolish Ivory's building in 1825. Some sources say that it had fallen into a bad state of repair; others that it could undergo no further enlargement or improvement for the convenience of its patrons and performers. The new Theatre Royal costing £6,000 was built on an adjacent site only a short distance from where the original had stood. On Easter Monday, 27th March 1826, it opened to the public with *The School for Scandal* followed by a farce called *Youth, Love, and Beauty.*

In 1903, the name was changed to the Norwich Hippodrome after the proprietor, Fred Morgan, had sold it to Bostock and Fitt, while he took over running the newly-built Grand Opera House in St Giles. For a year, the old theatre was a music hall staging variety shows. In 1904, Fred Morgan returned after selling the lease of the

Grand Opera House to Bostock and Fitt. They renamed their new acquisition the Norwich Hippodrome while Morgan restored the name Theatre Royal to its rightful place.

The Theatre Royal in the 1920s
This photograph shows part of the second building by William Wilkins in 1826

Fire claimed the theatre on Friday 22nd June 1934 but in a little over a year it had been rebuilt and reopened on 30th September 1935 with a performance of *White Horse Inn.*

A decade after the war, theatres came under threat from a new medium which brought top class entertainment right into the home - television. The 1950s and 1960s saw the death of many theatres throughout the country. Somehow the Theatre Royal just managed to survive, offering a diet of films, variety, pantomime and live all-in wrestling.

The Norwich Hippodrome closed during 1966 and it seemed as if the Theatre Royal would follow, but in May 1967 Norwich Council took the bold step of purchasing it at a cost of £90,000. After an inauspicious start the Theatre Royal began to grow under the guidance of administrators such as Laurence Hill and the flamboyant genius, Dick Condon, to become one of the most successful provincial theatres in the country.

There is no evidence now that a plain ever existed in Theatre Street. Buildings were demolished along all sides, the road was widened and the whole prospect looking towards the City Hall was opened up with a car park. This open space will disappear when the new Millennium Library is at last built to replace the old Central Library destroyed by fire on 1st August 1994.

And yet, looking at the fifty-three year old map surveying the chief buildings of historical and architectural interest before 1850, which accompanied the *City of Norwich Plan 1945*, Theatre Street appears to have had several worthy of note. Along the southern side of what was the narrowest section, an entire run of buildings from St Stephen's Church to Theatre Plain were marked in red, denoting that they were of major interest. Opposite, on the northern side, several buildings were marked in yellow showing that although they were of minor historic interest their design was good. All have gone in the name of progress and to ease the passage of the motor car.

UNIVERSITY PLAIN

A little over two miles from the centre of Norwich lies the most recent of the city's plains. It has appeared on the destination boards of local buses and is the postal address of several banks and shops on the campus. Yet it is hardly a plain in the usual Norwich sense of the word because in the space of thirty years it has been filled with modern buildings. The concrete complex which makes up the University of East Anglia stands on University Plain.

When the University opened in 1963, the administrative offices were housed in Earlham Hall, an elegant mansion dating from 1642, standing in its own parkland with a wide lawn sloping down to the river Yare. From the late eighteenth and through much of the nineteenth centuries, the Hall was rented by the Gurney family. Elizabeth Gurney, known to history as Elizabeth Fry the prison reformer, spent much of her childhood there.

Engraved by J.Acon, from a Drawing by J.S.Cotman, for the Excursions through Norfolk.

**Earlham Hall, an engraving from a drawing
by J.S.Cotman, 1819**

On a site adjacent to the historic Hall, construction of the University complex began during the 1960s on what had become known as University Plain. In this instance it seems as though the word plain was used to describe a building site!

'The architect is Denys Lasdun,' wrote Eric Fowler, 'who is fitting a remarkable concrete fabric into the beautiful wooded site, at the foot of which flows the upper stream of the river Yare.'

Part of the site had once been a golf course, opened in April 1932 and described in the Norwich Guide of 1934 as: 'A first-class 18-hole Municipal Golf Course...laid out amidst beautiful surroundings (and) should be used by every visitor to Norwich. The entrance to the Course is from Bluebell Road.' Evidence of the land's former use can still be seen in a few small mounds which once surrounded bunkers.

By October 1975, the first twelve-year phase had been completed. The administrative officers moved out of Earlham Hall and into the University's Administrative Centre. The Hall now houses the University's School of Law. During the following year, work began on the Sainsbury Centre For Visual Arts to house the Robert and Louisa Sainsbury collection and also to act as a venue for visiting exhibitions. The Sainsbury Collection consists of art from different cultures around the world, embracing both modern and ancient. The glass and aluminium structure won several awards for its designer, Sir Norman Foster, but some critics have likened it to a glorified aircraft hangar. It would certainly not look out of place at a modern airport.

Like the Sainsbury Centre, the rest of the campus does draw extreme views. Author James Wentworth Day, describing the University as it was during 1976, called it 'greenhouse architecture ... a hotch-potch of angular modernism.'

The concrete itself has not mellowed with age but has become stained by the elements and pollutants in the atmosphere. Yet for all its stark modernism, the ziggurats which house some of the student accommodation hark back, as the name implies, to the temples of ancient Mesopotamia. For those students fortunate enough to reside in them, they have an enviable outlook across the remains of the old golf course to the man-made broad with its reed-fringed bank and colonies of water birds.

University Plain has been transformed in thirty years into a city of learning, a twentieth century complex of functional buildings. But nowhere does it really lose sight of nature. The view across the Yare valley provides a spectacular backdrop that changes, almost imperceptibly, with the circle of the seasons. The grounds, too, are well maintained, plantations of trees breaking up the formal architectural lines. And amongst these stained, greying, concrete buildings are small squares - some of grass, some of tarmac - much like the plains of the old city a couple of miles away.

**Distant view of the University showing the
hangar-like Sainsbury Centre**